in-fulfillment.com
@in_fulfillment

ISBN: 979-8-218-17277-0

in fulfillment:
the designer's journey

justin dauer

cont

12

our impera-
tives

our values

10

32

ents

3 4 5

foreword

How we show up for people
and things we care about are
connected—by design, to our
values, our inner lives.

The more we find ways to be seen and understood the more siloed we seem to feel and become. We build language and narratives then co-op language and narratives to create assumed understandings.

The majority of our waking hours (I would say 'conscious,' but that feels like a bit of a reach) are spent at work. Whether we are working in our homes, shared workspaces, a company sponsored day dwelling, or Portugal.

No matter the physical proximity we have to our collaborators and colleagues, we seek connection. We need to be seen, acknowledged, valued, and to know that our time is being used purposefully. Increasingly we want to know that what we work towards will be aligned with our principles and furthermore to a legacy. That we will leave a legacy.

When we talk about legacy building it's often connected to fame, power, and privilege. We become mythical creatures that are either good or bad. There's no in between.

To have a legacy we need to be grand. We need our work to be noted and notable. We need to be beautiful creatures. We leave little room for our flawed humanity. We disregard the power of compound interest when it comes to good works and kindness. That our legacy can come from an accumulation of small acts.

Privilege is the ability to remove ourselves from the processes of equity and belonging when things get uncomfortable. Privilege allows for us to decide the scale of our sacrifice, whether real or perceived, based upon our level of irritation. We may want things to be different, but don't want to change ourselves.

I have mixed feelings about power. We've lived through flat power structures and open offices, in part, to move away from structural indications of power. I understand and can appreciate its purpose—and that power corrupts, or so the story goes. Leaders who don't do the inner work create destructive power dynamics fueled by a want to maintain and grow their strength.

In the positions of power that I've held, I saw my role as one of a protector and encourager for the growth and wellbeing of the people I've been entrusted with. This may seem like a backward approach. Executives and managers are supposed to be driven by projections and production. But, a people-first approach will drive profitability and the quality of all work produced. Power requires accountability and care.

I have discomfort with competition. Competition requires a winner and then there's everyone else. Competition consumes and can be fueled by some amount of data, but it's often tied to assumption and not minding our own business. We go beyond research and training and busy ourselves with what our competitors are doing. We measure ourselves against what we see and assume. Innovation doesn't live here.

I think we delude ourselves into thinking we need competition to do good work, to excel. This isn't to say that competitions, contests, awards, and accomplishments are bad by nature, but that being competitive doesn't need to be the driving force to push things forward. Constraints get us there.

How we show up for people and things we care about are connected—by design, to our values, our inner lives, the quality of our weekends and depth of our overall satisfaction...you know, all the things. How we show up as ourselves flows into the organizations we are a part of, becomes culture, ripple outward to clients and community, then circles back to us as individuals.

We are humans first and everything else second. Humans are hypocritical, iterative, ridiculous beings. These inherent qualities require grace, to be given and sought.

Erika Abrams
Founder, Scattered Good
Executive Director, Los Angeles Design Festival

For Kaity, who has helped me become
the best version of me.

.introduc-tion

The designer's legacy isn't built upon their choice of tools. The designer's legacy is built upon the choices they make—as macro and micro as that implies.

Twenty-five years.

It was just days before writing this Introduction when—for the first time in the **twenty-five years** of my career—I gave my first non-stumbly, confident self-introduction in a client meeting.

When I've given larger design conference presentations over the years, I've felt consistently confident in the delivery of my material, sprinkled with just the right amount of dad jokes (on second thought, there's probably no right amount of dad jokes). The stage, and the connection with people en masse, has consistently electrified me.

But consider the average *"Let's go around the room and introduce ourselves"* -caliber portion of any new client meeting. Without fail— despite having done this same routine for years as many of us have— I'd lose my proverbial footing when my turn came up, second-guessing myself throughout:

> *How much detail do I give? Should I mention how long I've been at this company? Do I need to say my last name, too? I'm not saying my title this time—wait, should I be saying it?*

Mental prep in advance be damned, the result: numerous tripped over words and awkward chuckles. So what changed?

The meeting I began with that took place a few days before writing this Introduction—a pre-sales conversation with a potential new client—was my first as the founder of Anomali, my design leadership consultancy. Anomali as a business was designed adopting my values, offering services to clients where I know I do my best work, existing in an environment I've cultivated to allow me to thrive and evolve. For the first time in my career, I'd hit that sweet spot trifecta:

1. Values-alignment
2. Work / work process-alignment
3. Environment-alignment

These three pillars equate to what informs my personal fulfillment. Leveraging implicit practices where I know I prosper—'proactivity,' 'big picture thinking,' and 'a need to build connection,' among them—I was operating in harmony with my personal, authentic narrative in that Anomali meeting. It's no coincidence that this effectively replicates the environment of fulfillment culled from engaging at a design conference. Those practices, and the values behind them, are consistent in both my personal and professional life.

Turning the lens inward: what fulfills you, inclusive of both sides of your personal and professional journey? Being challenged? Advocacy for others? Personal growth and evolution? Practices such as these are common to both spheres of existence. Conversely, what doesn't fulfill you? Recognizing when we're feeling disconnected from our work—e.g., going through the motions, sleepwalking—can be the first sign the bond is waning. That imperative connection: potentially severed. The cascading effects from this, and how to get out in front of them, will be a large part of the conversation we'll be having in this book.

When we're distinctly aware of where our fulfillment is derived from, we've taken a grand leap toward making meaningful work—work that connects to us as designers (nay, human beings), and to those who will ultimately engage with it. In a field of work largely comprised of impermanence (digital), the contrast is that our decisions can have lasting impact. Understanding this, in tandem with a clear value system, is essential to defining your legacy as a designer.

The designer's legacy isn't built upon their choice of tools. The designer's legacy is built upon the choices they make—as macro and micro as that implies. Legacy transcends 'us.' This is a mindset that takes us from 'me' to 'we' as we consider the bigger picture. There is a privilege and responsibility that are inherent in the craft. In communicating. In **connecting** with people through design.

Privilege and responsibility. Those notions are so vital (and evergreen) to our craft, and how we connect with other human beings. Formative, yet intrinsic to what we do. Every decision carries weight, and is bigger than us. We simply cannot foresee under what conditions people will be engaging with what we create. They need to be equitably understood, advocated for, and included along the way.

We create to connect. We create to advance. Leveraging our system of values as a North Star—and aligning to a role, team, and business whose own values compliment ours—ensures we're ever-mindful of the results of our actions through the choices we make. We're inserting meaning through action, our work a product of focused intent.

Agnostic of accolades, the tools we're using, or devoid of rushed procedure, the humble connection with those on the receiving end of what we're producing, and with those doing the producing, is imperative toward quality and evolution.

"Humble connection" is such a vital notion for a designer—yes, we may have years of applicable design study under our belt. Or the focused lab sessions from a UX bootcamp. Perhaps a lovely monogrammed portfolio of our work. But all that said: experience does not equal expert. If we're always students of our craft, we are also always making ourselves available to evolve.

As soon as we close our minds via an inner monologue of 'knowing it all', or branding ourselves a '#thoughtleader' on social media, the designer we **are** is our final form. The designer we **can be**, will never exist.

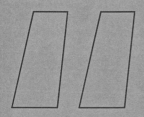

As soon as we close our minds via an inner monologue of 'knowing it all,' or branding ourselves a '#thoughtleader' on social media, the designer we <u>are</u> is our final form. The designer we <u>can be</u> will never exist.

"

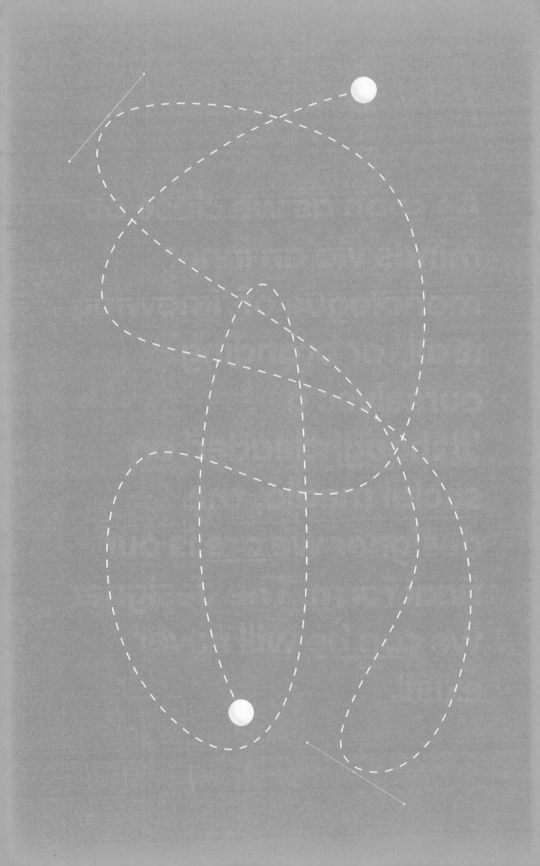

At the team level, leveraging the same values that are intrinsic to the work we create—humility, empathy, and respect among them—also gives designers a unique advantage in addressing so many of the cultural dynamics that can hinder evolution. Support of our teammates and the environment in which we create is equally as imperative as the advocacy we give to those we're designing for; designers are uniquely equipped to do exactly that by employing the exact same values and attributes intrinsic to our roles.

Work culture—part of the internal environment we exist within—forms the surrounding ecosystem to support our evolution as designers. In my first book, *Creative Culture: Human-Centered Interaction, Design, & Inspiration*, I wrote about the connection between us to our environment, us to each other, and us to the manner in which we create. Systems thinking is a core component of service design—going deeper into the dynamics of how things are interrelated, connected, and impact one other. To that end, *In Fulfillment: The Designer's Journey* zooms further into those systems of connection and dependence: us to our work, and our work to those who engage with it.

As a designer evolves over the years and course of their career, honest self-assessment toward derivation of self-reward will yield their best sense of personal—and creative—fulfillment. Does continuing to push the quality of their individual hands-on work scratch the itch? Or is a greater sense of being satiated derived via guiding the evolution of others and their work? It's about being respectful of, and honest toward, their journey in an eventual transition of fulfillment.

If that evolution takes a designer into a position of leadership, it's ever-paramount to maintain that value-driven core. Though their hands are no longer in motion, those values most certainly are: in actions over words. As with a designer leveraging their skill set toward the betterment of a work culture, the same logic applies toward leadership: humility, empathy, the act of setting expectations, proactive communication—all notions that apply to design (process) as much as they do to team leadership (practice). A design leader is functioning in the service of others and their evolution—a humble notion, for certain.

Leveraging personal narrative from a high school fascination with design through design leadership within a Fortune 5 business, we'll take a look at how **your own** narrative can develop around connection with what you create, and fulfillment in how you're creating it. We'll begin in the era of *Zoolander*, the first podcasts hitting your headphones, and skeuomorphism ceding to flat UI design...

chapter 1

our impera-tives

It's a gift to be challenged on our assumptions as it tears down self-imposed barriers, yielding greater connection. We get there by being perpetual students of our craft, always open to learning and evolving.

What is design, if not 'connection' made manifest?

In the early 2000s, a handful of years out of art school, I worked as a Creative Associate for a specialized technology company in Chicago. After the dot-com bubble burst and by way of a dire job market, this was my first non-freelance position in about a year. The role largely revolved around making surface-level design updates to the company's public-facing website. It was consistent yet unchallenging work. More often than not, I wasn't even busy. But, that said, having health insurance via full-time employment—and the ability to be consistently paid to do some basic design—was a comfort.

But comfort is not fulfillment.

Fulfillment means something different for everyone; fulfillment is personal. After a year or so in this position, the tradeoff of doing unfulfilling work began to take its toll on me and my design. The cultural issues that were prevalent on my team weren't helping. What's worse, I can assume my disconnection also began to take its toll on those who were engaging with the design I was putting into the world.

A sense of detachment set in; I was going through the motions, sleepwalking, and disconnected from my work. And 'going through the motions' in design, when there are people physically engaging with the experiences I was creating, was unacceptable; in my gut, I knew this.

During the course of my daily duties and through the cross-department relationships I made at the office, I became gradually more familiar with our authenticated web tools: account management dashboards, reporting mechanisms, etc.. Their interfaces were wanting, completely developer-built at the expense of an inherent design process or outside human engagement pre-deploy.

I felt that there was a business problem to be solved here—and a design wrong to be righted:

- What if those tools were thoughtfully designed?
- What if we engaged people in that design process, usability tested,

iterated, and made that process cyclical?
- How might quality, engagement, utilization, and sales be impacted?

These were delicious problems indeed, and I longed to solve them.

One evening after work, I formally acknowledged reality: I wasn't doing good work. I was disconnected, depressed, and unfulfilled. But I also knew there was a potential to synergize business opportunity (as it related to our web tools' interfaces) with a personal fulfillment that aligned with some of my core values: empathy, connection, and being challenged. And so, after a near-sleepless night, I awoke with a plan.

When I got to my desk in the morning, I emailed the CEO with some feedback and a pitch: there was a business opportunity with our web hosting tools that could lead to market differentiation, organic marketing, and increased sales. I laid out how an interface design team could directly address those issues. Then I hit 'Send.' If I received no reply, I knew I had at least tried; I would then give my two weeks and return to the feast-or-famine freelance work that at least afforded some fulfilling opportunities. That felt like the right thing to do.

I could see the CEO's glass-walled office from my cubicle. As he'd occasionally step out to traverse the open floor plan, I'd wonder if he'd head in my direction. Though, maybe he was behind on emails and wouldn't see what I'd sent for a week, or a month? Or perhaps he'd just delete it?

Around noon as I was looking at my monitors, I heard someone behind me say, *"Want to get some lunch?"* It was the CEO in all his C-level splendor. I eked out some form of affirmation that I did, in fact, want to get some lunch. As I grabbed my coat, my boss, who sat in the cubicle behind me, said, *"You're going to lunch with him?"* Yeah... I guess I was.

We took a short walk to the Walnut Room, a restaurant built in 1907 inside Marshall Field's (now Macy's) on State Street in downtown Chicago. He got right to it, asking me to tell him more about my idea. In response, I just went for it: I walked through the concept of an interface design team to directly address the issues I'd cited: promote human connection, greater adoption, and word of mouth. He recognized that our web hosting tools weren't well-designed, which ended up directly impacting the call center due to errors and overall confusion, an insight I wasn't aware of. We agreed that putting an intuitive design process in place to reduce these friction points was a trackable effort; data-informed design decisions would further ease those burdens and promote increased usage.

Our walk back into the office was a literal and metaphorical transformation: I was now the business' first Lead Interface Designer, tasked with building a team (I'd never managed anyone before!) and establishing the very process I'd articulated. To say I had an Alec Guinness *"my god, what have I done"* -caliber moment would be apt, but renewed hope married with creative fulfillment was my dominant mindset.

In my new role, I met different and incredible people within the organization and forged new relationships. I began building a team, and we integrated with development to design (and redesign) products, with human beings at the forefront of our process. Getting Human Factors International-trained in usability testing further added to my applicable skill set and ensured our group could engage, iterate, improve, and connect.

This design work fulfilled me and, in tandem, bettered the business' products. And the quality of my work exponentially increased, as it was directly aligned with my values.

transcending medium

Thanks for joining me for that stroll down memory lane. It's a story that's as much about the perils of **disconnection** as it is about the inverse. Not every decision needs to be as grand as writing an email to the CEO—recognizing your potential disconnection is where your own story can begin.

Now let's move up to the present day.

Since 2018 I've been working with UX Hong Kong co-founders Dan Szuc and Jo Wong on their Make Meaningful Work (MMW) framework.

MMW is about taking the work we do and ensuring we do it with purpose and intention, adding meaning to what we create. A lot of people at various stages of their careers (entry-level through C-level) tend to go through a phase called 'sleepwalking,' where they're doing things that are routine, easy, comfortable, and utterly unfulfilling. Sound familiar? They're not developing new skills and not making the impact they want to have. Through observation, tools, and trackable micro exercises, MMW aims to move people from sleepwalking to connection with their work, themselves, and their environment. 'Sparkle,' as the program puts it.

It's a fascinating concept that we'll touch on with greater depth in the next chapter. By moving beyond sleepwalking and the resulting detachment from our work, and identifying and leveraging what fulfills us, we can sparkle.

That's a beautiful notion, but as we all know, fulfillment is not just contextualized by our professional lives. Pause for a moment to think about what fulfills you **away** from a business context. What satiates you to your core and aligns with your sense of self?

For example, is it:

- The act of helping people?
- Learning from your mistakes?
- Utilizing your gifts?
- Giving back?

What happens if you're consistently deprived of those things? Are you able to sleep soundly at night, or do you find yourself staring at the ceiling as if something is missing? These example points of fulfillment have a commonality and a connection: their relevance to our personal and professional lives.

It's an extensible concept: there's the idea that the 'self' we bring into the office (personal) cannot be divorced from the one that exists within the office (professional)—bringing our 'whole self' into work, or our 'true self,' as it's called. There's a distinct value to this mindset, as explained by *Bring Your Whole Self to Work* author Mike Robbins in his Forbes magazine interview:

> *"Bringing our whole selves to work means showing up authentically, leading with humility, and remembering that we're all vulnerable, imperfect human beings doing the best we can."*

Conversely, when we do the opposite—or the work culture is prohibitive—Robbins notes the adverse effects as well as the (personal + business) value that is inherently lost:

> *"When we don't bring our whole selves to work we suffer – lack of engagement, lack of productivity, and our well-being is diminished. We aren't able to do our best, most innovative work, and we spend and waste too much time trying to look good, fit in, and do or say the "right" thing. For teams and organizations, this lack of psychological safety makes it difficult for the group or company to thrive and perform at their highest level because people are holding back some*

of who they really are."

That lack of engagement—**disconnection**, really—is a direct result of being unable to be our true selves in both spheres of existence: personal and professional. Our quality of life suffers, just as our quality of work does when we are not satiated. Fulfilling common core values in one sphere of existence, but compromising in another, can have ripple effects with dire consequences. How?

For designers, disconnection can yield visual communication (connection) breakpoints between designer and user that inhibit quality at potentially crucial interaction points. Design, UX, and all its permutations are not disciplines where we can 'phone it in,' so to speak, since we can never assume people are going to be engaging with what we create under idyllic circumstances:

- Is someone engaging with our experience while holding a smartphone with one hand on the subway?
- Are they interacting with a vital workflow in the midst of a crisis?
- Or are they managing account information on an archaic terminal on a noisy factory floor?

The possibilities are factually infinite.

Every design decision carries weight, and is bigger than us. It's a notion that reveals a distinct truth: being **personally** fulfilled also has direct implications upon **those we're creating for**. Sleepwalking is not an option. And when we're disconnected from our process and work, the privilege and responsibility of connecting with people is on the line.

understanding the privilege and responsibility of connection

Thirty-ish years ago, when *Batman Returns* was at the movies and Stone Temple Pilots' 'Plush' crunched heavy chords on the radio, I was a sophomore in high school. One afternoon while in school I saw something that changed my life: the album cover designs the Graphic Design 1 class had made, now on display in the back of my study hall. My mom was a trained fine artist whose paintings and illustrations had marveled me since childhood, but these album covers had something else going on that drew me in.

I approached the study hall faculty member and asked about the pieces; she said it was her class' work. I had only taken fine art classes to that point, but those covers resonated with me: it was art but visually communicating.

Inspired by what I had seen and now heard, I asked if I could take her class. She made the point that this wasn't fine art, but set my expectations on what they **did** do in design:

"We're visually problem solving."

Rather than dissuade me, that response made me hungrier to learn.

I worked Design 1 into my schedule the following semester. It was hands-on, low-fidelity, pencil / ink / scissors-type work, and it was absolutely amazing. The manually inked and stenciled-on letterforms, the texture and weight of various paper stocks, color usage, and overall visual communication—I felt like something awakened inside of me that transcended mere 'satisfaction.' I've had very few moments of absolute clarity in my life, but this was one of them: design was what satiated me. This was **it**.

Scaling back a little over the next couple of years on my other favorite pastimes (playing *Street Fighter 2* and reading comics), I immersed myself both in books on design as well as the projects we were assigned. I had a renewed focus: assembling a strong, diverse portfolio of work to get into art school. My design and fine art teachers selflessly helped me assemble the most successful pieces.

Ultimately attending The School of the Art Institute of Chicago's 'Immediate Decision Option' day—a morning in which you present your portfolio of work to faculty members, finding out if you've been accepted by the afternoon—I was accepted into their Visual Communications program. There, over the next four years, I learned and evolved. And I was fueled by the masters: Gropius. Müller-Brockmann. Sutnar.

"

Be it a concert venue poster, a website, or an app icon, design is solving the problem of engaging people, agnostic of their circumstances, to connect and convey an experience.

"

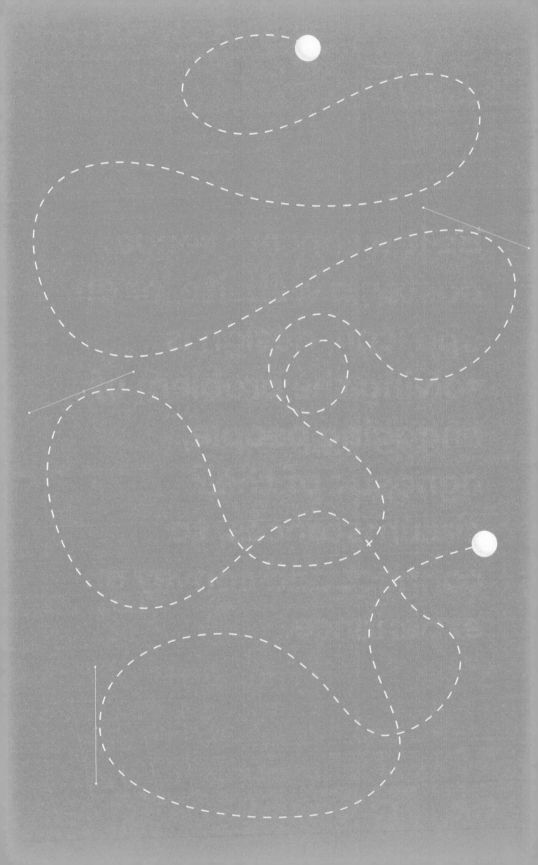

Through their work across architecture, typography, and information design, I began to understand the privilege and responsibility inherent in the craft, in communicating and connecting with people through all forms of design.

Privilege and responsibility. Internalizing and understanding the significance of those concepts—and how they apply to how and what we create—is imperative to our craft. Why? Be it a concert venue poster, a website, or an app icon, design is solving the problem of engaging people, agnostic of their circumstances, to connect and convey an experience.

The privilege, then, is that we are in the important position of being the facilitators to foster that connection, whatever the respective medium might be. Given that, it's our responsibility to ensure we engage with people at our best and most fulfilled. It means we must craft with awareness, mindful of what our environment provides and what we're putting back into it. Or, if you climb the hierarchical echelon to have management responsibilities: how you build a practice of meaningful engagement to ensure your team can do the same.

understanding white privilege in design

In tandem with the privilege of connecting with people through design, there's also the privilege of being a designer—in particular, being a **white** designer. And it's our responsibility to center equity in how we create, as inclusively and wide-lensed as possible, every time we pick up a pencil, wire a frame, co-design and collaborate, usability test and iterate.

In a sobering stat shared in the 2021 "AIGA Design POV Research Reports," our industry's lacking diversity is laid bare:

> *"...in the U.S., the Design community under indexes on Black/African Americans (4.9% vs. 12.6% in the labor force), Hispanics/Latinxs (9.0% vs. 18.0%)..."*

The design industry is predominantly white (80 percent in the U.S., per the AIGA report), and white privilege is thus prevalent—consciously and subconsciously. Homogeneous thinking, process, planning, and creation can be extensive in what is designed and how it's designed.

> *"[Privilege is] a gift that you did nothing to earn. The benefits depend on the context."* — George Aye, co-founder of Greater Good Studio, from his talk 'Design Education's Big Gap: Understanding the Role of Power'

I recognize my own bias and privilege as a white male (in life, as well as in design). Nonetheless, I've gotten a lot wrong along the way and very likely still do. Humility, which we'll discuss in depth in this book, is essential toward recognizing where we've gotten it wrong on inclusion in the past. Learning—translated to actionable change—is the next vital step based on that recognition.

Being challenged on our assumptions is in the DNA of our craft. For the fellow white folks reading this book: the world's use cases can't be defined by our privileged lens. The design teams and organizations I've built have been designed to be representative of the world we're creating for: diverse, non-homogenous backgrounds and perspectives. If we're genuinely trying to connect with other people, it literally can't be any other way—lest the empathy we preach in our design process become a value without substance in practice and output.

Removing white privilege-based barriers to equitable engagement means equal access to those who often aren't given a voice in the process, **but must be.**

removing barriers

I opened this chapter with the question *"What is design, if not 'connection' made manifest?"*

This notion applies as much to us and our work (internal connection) as it does to our work and those who engage with it (external connection). And if 'design' and 'connection' are effectively synonymous, ensuring that the bond is barrier-free must be an essential value to drive us. Nothing can stand in the way of its access.

For the internal connection, that, of course, means fulfillment via our design. When we are not detached, our work's quality and inclusion of bigger-picture concerns become less of a hurdle and a more organic (yet strategic) outcome.

We can give better focus to that value through the external connection: 'access for all' means we're inclusively ensuring everyone can engage with what we're creating. We just discussed how this applies to white privilege in design and equitable engagement. We're leveling the playing field by not being exclusionary in our creation(s) through the design process or by the artifact created. This is also the definition of empathy for those who are differently abled than we may be, removing the bias we can introduce by not seeing beyond our personal use case.

The privilege and responsibility of design.

Looking closer, the Interaction Design Foundation cites some common barriers users can have:

- *Visual (e.g., color blindness)*
- *Motor/mobility (e.g., wheelchair-user concerns)*
- *Auditory (hearing difficulties)*
- *Seizures (especially photosensitive epilepsy)*
- *Learning/cognitive (e.g., dyslexia)*

Ability barriers can also arise for any user:

- *Incidental (e.g., sleep deprivation)*

- *Environmental (e.g., using a mobile device underground)*
  The possibilities regarding who might be trying to access your
  product/service are virtually limitless.

'Virtually limitless' is an entirely apt summary of the potential
use cases inclusive of barriers, physically as well as situationally. This
aligns with what I noted earlier regarding why we can't assume people
will engage with what we create under idyllic condition.

You may have heard the phrase 'meeting people where they're at'
in design and technology-centric solutions; it means you're creating
flexible and thoughtful experiences to fairly engage people agnostic of
conditions. For us, this is an opportunity: what could be more fulfilling
than ensuring that what we create can be engaged with by all people
fairly and equally?

There are process-centric means to facilitate that connection—with
those we're creating for, the environment they exist within, and how
time contributes to its usage, efficacy, and impact. By being inclusive
of the very people we're creating for in our design process, while
being mindful of the bigger picture of environmental impact, we're
generating that imperative connection to remove barriers.

For example, participatory design (or co-design), client workshops,
discovery / research / observation, and usability testing are all
methods of including those we're creating for in our overall design
process and going deeper into the implications of our decisions. This
act of going deeper generates connection and manifests itself both

internally and externally:

- **For us:** our own fulfillment via empathy for those we're creating for yields a personal connection to our work. It's 'doing the right thing' by also doing right by people and their environment, thus removing the barrier potentially caused by our own disconnection.
- **For our work:** its connection to those we're designing for by being inclusive in how we create. By understanding—and collaborating with—those who will engage with our design, an intuitive and accessible experience can result.

Diverse, non-homogenous insights culled from a 'me-to-we' mindset break us out of our silos and remove our blinders. It's a gift to be challenged on our assumptions as it tears down self-imposed barriers, yielding greater connection. We get there by being perpetual students of our craft, always open to learning and evolving.

When our sense of connection is at its strongest, our personal values are also at their most fulfilled. That bond is no coincidence: recognizing how powerfully that value system drives our fulfillment throughout our career is where we'll go next.

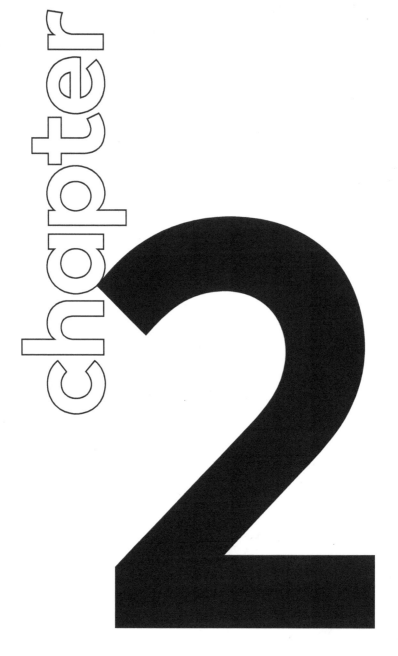

chapter

2

our values

An introspective look at the scenarios in your life that have yielded the most fulfillment will provide a direct window into your most cherished values.

As we discussed last chapter, the greatest feeling of being 'at odds' (unfulfilled) with our design emerges when it does not align with our system of values.

But you might say, *"Well no, Justin, I'm detached from my work because it's just plain boring and unchallenging."* In that example sentiment, however, your values—and how they're not being addressed—are still front and center.

Values are anything you deem important to you, as they apply to the way you live and your design. They're your North Star in determining your sense of fulfillment, informing your life's priorities, and ultimately driving your contentment.

their identification

Before we can begin aligning our values to our work, we first need to be able to define them. In fact, we've already gotten a head start on this process: in the first chapter, I asked you to consider what fulfills you away from a business context, using these examples as question starters:

- The act of helping people?
- Learning from your mistakes?
- Utilizing your gifts?
- Giving back?

Leveraging that same list, let's look deeper at what values drive fulfillment in these cases:

The act of helping people
Have you ever stopped to give someone directions when asked rather than just pass them by? Why did you feel compelled to help?

Perhaps it's because you've been that person before, knowing what it feels like to need assistance and understanding that it can be hard to ask for it. Putting yourself in someone else's shoes to understand how they feel is all about demonstrating **empathy**.

Learning from your mistakes
We all make mistakes; *"to err is human,"* as Alexander Pope wrote. There are effectively two ways to respond to a misstep, however: we process, learn, and evolve, or we let the opportunity slip and cyclically repeat the error. You focus on improvement, mindful of your evolution: this is all about **growth**.

Utilizing your gifts
Sometimes a straightforward task, chore, or project feels good to take care of. We have a lot to do, and checking items off a list (metaphorical or literal) can be fulfilling in and of itself. Other times, being tested satisfies something deeper: running a marathon. Building furniture. Putting together a complex puzzle. You appreciate leveraging your gifts and pushing yourself to employ them: this is all about **challenge**.

Giving back
The oxytocin boost we get from volunteering our time to important causes is no coincidence: giving back feels good. You've always looked beyond yourself and did your part to better other people's

(and the world's) conditions. This is all about **making a difference**.

An introspective look at the scenarios in your life that have yielded the most fulfillment will provide a direct window into your most cherished values. And sometimes, you'll be able to spot patterns based on common themes that can yield logical groupings. For example: if respect, connection, and empathy are three values you identify, then you could qualify being 'people-first' as one of your essential values.

their prioritization

When looking for a best-fit role for us and our work, it's essential to be crystal clear on our most important values. As such, being able to prioritize them is vital. This allows us to have a clear sense of the 'must-haves' for the respective design work itself and the given role, the given organization, and the process by which they create. Sometimes, the work will satisfy some values more than others, making it even more imperative that you weigh what you need against what you could potentially function without (or with a diminished capacity).

For example, could you take on design work that made a user's workflow more intuitive (strong on 'empathy' and 'connection') but was part of a larger SaaS product built upon capitalistic goals (not so strong on 'making a difference')? When we're unclear on our most important values, we may take on work and roles that drive disconnection over time. So, take some 'you' time to think through which of your values have most fulfilled you over the course of your life, personal and professional.

Now we've all likely been part of a forced ranking-type workshop exercise during our careers. Done in a group setting, this exercise revolves around concepts or themes on a whiteboard, with those in the room assigning priority to each by putting a star or a dot near it. At the end of the exercise, the group can see which concepts have the most stars/dots, yielding a broad consensus on what's most important to the environment, people, project, or business. This result creates a distinct order: a plan of attack, features for an MVP (and what to work on first), etc.

Take the spirit of this exercise as a solo initiative, since you know your values best, and force a ranking on them. Perhaps by giving them a score based on how intensely fulfilled you felt by each over the years and experiences. Forced ranking is not easy; in any workshop setting, it never is. So go easy on yourself as you work through it.

The beautiful thing is that your prioritized values can then be leveraged in so many ways:

- Informing which questions you ask during your next job interview
- Serving as an objective gut check when you feel the connection to your work waning.
- Determining if the business you're employed by is operating in unison with what's most important to you.

their ethnical symbiosis

An October 2020 survey by The Creative Group and AIGA noted a staggering 88 percent of currently employed designers (and 56 percent of unemployed ones) said they would not accept a position with a company whose values did not align with their personal ones.

Taken from AIGA's 2021 report "Design POV: An In-Depth Look at the Design Industry Now," the information goes deeper into designers' expectations:

> *"As designers think about the future, they believe the community should have a Point of View (a position the profession stands for) about: Advancing Diversity, Equity, Inclusion and Accessibility (DEIA); creating standards for the Design profession; advocating for Design; strengthening the Design community; advancing Design education/ learning; being a force for change; advancing purposeful/ethical business practices; supporting freelancers, solopreneurs and small businesses; promoting sustainability/environmental responsibility."*

Given that, let's take a look at how your chosen organization's ethics—where you design and evolve—aligns with your values across things like:

- **what** they're building (product)

- **how** they're building it (design process)
- **why** they're building it (purpose)
- **who** is impacted by the build (clients, users, the environment, and you)

Ethics are a code of conduct based on a set of morals geared mainly toward business and business processes, including the design process. How a business approaches dynamics like the above list defines its ethics and, in practice, will pertain to both internal/cultural things (transparency, diversity, fairness) and external/end-user things (product privacy, 'customer-first,' environmental responsibility).

Values, however, are personal. How they're imprinted upon a business to inform its code of ethics can largely be attributed to those who founded it. The book *Principles of Management* cites a well-known example:

> "A company's culture, particularly during its early years, is inevitably tied to the personality, background, and values of its founder or founders, as well as their vision for the future of the organization. When entrepreneurs establish their own businesses, the way they want to do business determines the organization's rules, the structure set up in the company, and the people they hire to work with them. For example, some of the existing corporate values of the ice cream company Ben & Jerry's Homemade Holdings Inc. can easily be traced to the personalities of its founders Ben Cohen and Jerry

Greenfield. In 1978, the two high school friends opened up their first ice-cream shop in a renovated gas station in Burlington, Vermont. Their strong social convictions led them to buy only from the local farmers and devote a certain percentage of their profits to charities. The core values they instilled in their business can still be observed in the current company's devotion to social activism and sustainability, its continuous contributions to charities, use of environmentally friendly materials, and dedication to creating jobs in low-income areas."

So, what is the interplay between those two spheres, business ethics and what's important to you, as it pertains to your fulfillment?

When we talk about ethics and morals, we're talking about what's right and wrong. Good and bad. The 'bad' of certain business decisions can be diametrically opposed to your set of values, causing friction with (and ultimately detachment from) your work. Let's go back to that example list cited in our 'identifying your values' exercise to see what this might look like.

The act of helping people = empathy

In the above point, we discussed how you might hold empathy as one of your values; if UX is your discipline of design, there's a good chance that's the case. For your external work, it's essential to connect with, understand, and advocate for those you're creating for to best design something that meets their needs. For internal interactions, that same value applies to how you engage and collaborate with your teammates; empathy and respect go hand-in-hand.

For example, let's consider: what if the content delivery mechanism that a community-based product you were working on was predicated upon targeting people with ads containing intentionally false or misleading information? You may be solving complex UX issues to provide an intuitive experience, but this piece of potential portfolio material is effectively coming at the expense of what's important to you as a person as well as the human beings it will ultimately harm or deceive.

And what of the internal environment surrounding this work? Was the design team pushed to the limit to hit a fixed release cadence or sprint milestone? Were people working hours at the expense of their personal lives, self-care, or overall well-being? When shareholder appeasement supersedes the human condition, not only do the creators themselves burn out but imperative design processes also often get reduced or removed altogether; empathy and respect be damned.

No product appears out of thin air: there's always an entire design process and project lifecycle surrounding it. Consider what we mentioned at the end of the first chapter about boundary-free design: access for all. As a value, we could consider this equality. At the product level, this would translate to greater reach; it would also mean supporting processes around it, including more time spent testing, refining, developing, and debugging behind the scenes.

Inclusive design is at the heart of an ethical design process, but not every business (or product) is willing to put the rigor (inclusive of time and resources) behind it. The humans or other living creatures on the other side of the experience become collateral damage. Since this sits at odds with your values, we need to consider your options and consequences: it's up to us to advocate for what's right and aligns with our values and then educate the business on how that translates into value for them (for example, boundary-free design equals greater product reach).

Sometimes change isn't feasible, thanks to business direction, management, commitments, or a myriad of other potential reasons. When there's such a fundamental mismatch in ethics versus values, detachment will set in. Your needs—what's important to you—are not being fulfilled. In going through the motions your quality of work will suffer. Anything potentially portfolio-worthy will have come at the expense of your sense of self as much as the human beings who engage with what you've designed.

So consider this: are those corporate beliefs painted on the wall in the cafeteria and screen-printed on corporate swag just lip service? Or are they exhibited in actual demonstrable actions, saturated in culture and design process? Most importantly: do they align with what you hold sacred? Your fulfillment, your work, and those on the receiving end are all on the line.

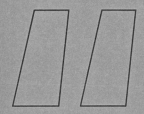

It's up to us to advocate for what's right and aligns with our values and then educate the business on how that translates into value for them (for example, boundary-free design equals greater product reach).

their utility

One of the beautiful facets of a given value is that it's effectively timeless. When you peel back the layers on why [x] fulfills you as it's applied to various (personal or work) dynamics over the course of your life, you'll realize that the value itself has been a constant.

For example, I released the 2nd edition of *Creative Culture*, a book largely about the synergies between a healthy, people-first culture and design process, in June 2020. The book focused on engagement, interaction, and inspiration, primarily driven by tangible and in-person spatial dynamics. In essence, it was the articulated culmination of years of experience.

As we all know, 2020 was the year the COVID-19 pandemic forever altered our way of work and life. Millions of workers went remote full-time on short notice, with culture and process shifting to being driven by video calls and collaboration apps. Given that, how did a book about in-person and tangible dynamics fare, given an unforeseen global shift to remote working and digital collaboration? Actually, quite well.

Because the methods and themes are all built upon a system of values, the approaches were applicable agnostic of office or home office. For example:

Consider how businesses, by and large, welcome new employees: typically on a Monday, often in cattle call format, sometimes spending the day in orientation, and perhaps even by lobbing them right into project work with little context to go on. This formulaic, impersonal approach falls short of demonstrating the **respect**, **connection**, and **empathy** a business or team needs to convey to the new employee who just entrusted them with their success and professional evolution.

There's a better way to welcome a new team member. I prefer to welcome them on a Friday, so a different kind of momentum (from a Monday–Friday span) is produced. It's an energy generated by putting the individual first and making the welcoming experience personal over clinical. The dynamic is less cattle call, more one-to-one dialogue-driven, and teeing up the weekend directly after is no coincidence.

As I wrote in *Creative Culture*:

"Why do I care so much about an employee's first day when, in reality, it's a micro-fraction of their entire career? The fact of the matter is this: the consideration a company gives to how an employee is welcomed and brought into the fold speaks volumes as to what lies ahead.

After the ink is dry and logistics have been discussed, I arrange with our new team member to start with us on a Friday ... many of us have likely become accustomed to first day Monday's; the prevailing thought being that consistency and momentum are inherent in a consecutive five-day workweek. And there is. That said, I'm looking for a different kind of momentum: one that's predicated upon time for reflection, which only carrying through the weekend will supply. What follows is a process that's as finely tuned as it is organic. There are no client deliverables or billable work on tap today. Instead, I've laid out a series of events designed to acclimate my new team member as a valued human being, brimming with ideas and creativity."

I call this Friday 'The New Day One.' Every aspect is designed around connecting with the new team member and demonstrating my respect for them as a unique individual. When they arrive, my butt is out of my seat and I'm greeting them at the door. We've all been in that situation where you enter a business's office on your first day and, not knowing anyone, immediately feel 'small.' My intent is to put myself in their shoes and ensure that they feel welcomed.

When it's time for lunch, I'm not searching for a place to take them at the last minute, ultimately finding a location where it's too loud to converse. Instead, a venue is pre-selected (based on vetted knowledge of its suitability) and pre-reserved in advance.

The culmination of the day—which I call the 'Inspiration' portion— occurs when I ask the new team member to take me someplace in the city that inspires them. Via their chosen location and in physically venturing away from the office, I'm able to gain insight into them as an individual that transcends what folio work can yield:

- What physical aspects of their selected location have impacted who they are?
- How did it inspire their way of creating or approaching problems?

Understanding the impact of spatial dynamics on an individual is vital toward an individualistic, yet ultimately holistic, view of who they are.

So how can a day revolving around tangible dynamics—meeting a new employee at the door, broadly ensuring they feel welcome, going to a physical location that inspires them—apply in a pandemic-driven, imposed remote work year?

Consider this message I received on Twitter from Andy P. Browne, who had just welcomed a new teammate during that timeframe {FIG 1}.

Exclusively leveraging digital tools, Andy and his team recreated the Inspiration part of The New Day One to demonstrate **respect**, **connection**, and **empathy**—the same values that fuel the in-person version of the experience:

- **Respect**: taking the time during the work day—pausing with intent—to engage with their new teammate as a human being
- **Connection**: going deeper than the surface level to understand who this person is, why they create, and what fuels them to do what they do
- **Empathy**: putting themselves in the new teammate's shoes to

FIG 1: @DTAndyB's Tweet reveals an exensibility of approach for The New Day One

make sure they feel included, understood, and appreciated via the remote Inspiration experience

And to the other dynamics of in-person New Day One connection, leveraging similar values also inform a remote version of welcoming:

- Instead of meeting the new teammate at the door, I personally welcome them virtually via a video call in the morning, reserving time explicitly for this interaction
- Instead of introducing them to the team in person, I ask the team to reach out individually to virtually introduce themselves
- Instead of taking them out to lunch, we gather as a team for a video call post-lunch (so a medium-sized group of people isn't collectively self-conscious from watching each other eat) to casually converse and connect

So despite *Creative Culture*'s leveraging of specific connection-based values in a tangible sense, they are as clear as day. As such, the methods which serve as their delivery mechanism are portable between in-office and remote work. When your values are at the core of [x]—from an in-person or remote first day, zooming out to as grand a notion as life's fulfillment or a career's fulfillment—you'll end up in a place that feels true to yourself and your beliefs.

their necessity toward making meaningful work

Early in chapter one, we talked about Make Meaningful Work, or MMW for short.

Now let's be frank: 'framework' can be a swear word. Not every system is appropriate for every (stated) scenario across design, development, project management and onward, we need to make **it** work for **us**, not vice versa. Further, some are more about the sale than the substance. And even further than that: some are flat-out bullshit.

Bound to its DNA, however, MMW is a platform driven by us rather than the inverse. It employs a tool called Practice Spotting™, where we leverage the power of personal narrative—our own stories—to identify where we thrive and connect best and what potential barriers there might've been along the way (an approach I'm often employing in this book). We're able to define patterns that help us discover the values we want to embody in the environment in which we work.

A sense of narrative and storytelling are key skills for designers to have in their toolkits. From the job interview process to presenting your work, articulating your process, how you contributed, and the outcomes are vital in connecting with your audience and bringing them along for the ride. You can further organically develop those skills as you leverage MMW.

I like to call it the 'fulfillment platform,' but it's much deeper than that. As the book *Make Meaningful Work: From Sleepwalking to Sparkle* articulates:

"Distractions can shift our focus away from project tasks that we need to complete to achieve meaningful outcomes. They also create environments and cultures in which we might fall prey to transactional practices that leave us little room to pause, take stock and reflect on what is most important: the work that we are doing together and how we interact and relate with each other while doing that work.

We discovered that most of us want to spend more time on meaningful work and work with teams that are engaged in making that happen. Projects where our skills and practice strengths are working well together that encourage us to learn, improve and thrive.

We call this Sparkle.
Sparkle does not always translate to happiness. Rather it's an energy related to being in flow, engaged, thriving and focused on what intrinsically motivates you, your team and organization.

When we do Practice Spotting™, we are looking for both the explicit and implicit practices in the stories people share. By doing Practice Spotting™ we are able to look at the context from various or different perspectives including people, time and place. This includes the good, the bad and all the degrees in between and the learnings in the interactions and relationships between people."

Leveraging the practices we spot back into our work, professional relationships, and cultural dynamics at the office, we then track their efficacy through practical micro exercises week-over-week. This process is powered by tools to help us understand how to insert meaning into our work—documentable and evolving artifacts that give focus to our fulfillment. Let's take a look at some of them.

One of the cornerstone tools is called a Character Card. A Character Card's purpose is to help you build your character by clarifying what drives you, what's important to you, and helping you understand your values so they can be projected forward in your life and your work. For example, this is what my card looks like filled out {FIG 1.1}.

We best utilize the value of the card via a simple act: applying it to telling our own stories, based on our own experiences, developing our own personal narrative. Just like how aligning a persona to a journey map can bring a workflow to life, the same notion applies here.

In the midst of the hustle of a typical workday, how do we bring you into a space that lets you begin to leverage these cards? By employing what MMW calls the Sparkle Studio: a physical or virtual space where we make a deliberate energy shift in contrast to the busy workday's. Think of it like a deliberate act of slowing down—pausing with intent—

Justin
NAME

DRAW YOURSELF

Philosophy on work :
1. We must stay humble to evolve (us + our work)
2. Fulfillment is essential, and is bigger than us
3. Design to facilitate connection
4. People first

Philosophy on relationships :
1. Mutual respect is the cornerstone
2. Pro-active communication leaves no one guessing
3. Empathy fuels connection
4. Diverse perspectives over homogenous thinking

Impact on the world :
1. Help grow, support, and facilitate the evolution of others
2. Create to connect over performative execution
3. Evolve office culture to support / engage
4. Actions over words to set a lasting example

© www.makemeaningfulwork.com 2021

FIG 1.1: My completed Character Card

in a collegial, creative environment. Like a writer's room session married with a coffee chat.

It's here where you'll leverage different lenses to inform diverse perspectives across your stories. You'll begin to develop daily micro exercises that compliment your work, and your interactions, to help inform where you best thrive. Those micro exercises begin with Practice Spotting™, and it's what brings this all together.

As I mentioned, Practice Spotting™ is an observational and sense-making tool that enables you to challenge your assumptions, gain depth into what fulfills you, and uncover the hidden learning opportunities from your personal and professional journey.

The Spotting Card is the artifact where we leverage one of our own personal stories to go deeper, looking at the implicit and explicit practices within and breaking down one of them to better understand how it fuels us, our connection, our work, and our fulfillment.

I'll use one of my own stories as an example here so we can look at how this all congeals. We'll go back to the story I shared to start the book: me as a young designer and my interaction with the CEO of the company.

If you recall, I was going through a period of disconnection. Then, I saw what I perceived as an opportunity with our business and products and decided based on what I thought was right. So what did I actually, tangibly do in a transactional sense? Take a look at the Explicit Practices in the filled-out Spotting Card {FIG 1.2}.

- I observed a perceived business need
- I made a decision on my direction (personally, by my work, with the company)
- I wrote an email

Behind the scenes and driving those tangible actions: I made a connection (sending the email) to facilitate a change and, hopefully, potential impact for myself, my work, our products, and our business. These "behind the scenes" initiatives are called Implicit Practices, and it's where our eyes should next focus on that Spotting Card:

- Proactivity: *I didn't wait for opportunity to fall in my lap.*
- Reflection: *I looked inward.*
- Connect what I do to the business (bigger picture): *I saw a potential opportunity for our products and my skill set.*
- To engage, begin with action: *I had to take the first step to make anything happen.*
- Growing a consciousness (self-awareness): *I acknowledged my design quality wasn't where it needed to be.*
- Honesty to self: *I was realistic about my disconnection.*
- Looking beyond self: *I realized the impact of my disconnection was bigger than me.*

Now look to the right on the Spotting Card, where we'll go deeper by breaking down one of those Implicit Practices: both its enablers

FIG 1.2: The Spotting Card revealing Explicit and Implicit Practices

and the barriers we (may have) encountered along the way. In this example, I chose 'to engage, begin with action.'

Vulnerability and honesty with ourselves are critical here so we can best understand a barrier-free relationship with our values and what fulfills us. To take the first step to making anything happen, I needed to believe in myself, allow my need to evolve to serve as a guide, and put myself in the shoes of those who were likely impacted by my disconnection. These **enablers** helped propel me forward.

In tandem, I can look back and recognize the fear I had that was in play during that time. *What if I put myself out there and failed? What if my email was deleted, I was chastised, or ignored completely?* As George McFly remarked in the Hill Valley High School cafeteria way back in 1955: *"I don't know if I could take that kind of rejection."* On the other side of that coin, what if the change I sought worked out, but I did not have the mettle to be up to the (new) tasks at hand? 'Be careful what you wish for,' defined. These **barriers** nearly kept me in a frozen state of comfort over fulfillment, known quantity versus the great unknown.

By documenting these enablers and barriers, I can connect and contextualize them into other scenarios within my cultural interactions, life, and work. To make these exercises actionable and valuable, we can track and measure to see how this depth into my fulfillment can be projected outward to other dynamics. This is brought to fruition via the last artifact I want to talk about: the Practice Card {FIG 1.3}.

We'll pick one practice from that Spotting Card that we'd like to explore and create a micro exercise, a dynamic that isn't totally new but something we want to try and approach differently, to practice on and measure. By leveraging a practice from my narrative—empathy in this example—I'm directly applying something that fulfills me to a team relationship dynamic. For example, letting others talk first in meetings; collaboration over oration.

Let's say I was experiencing an adversarial relationship with another team within the same organization. Going into design reviews, the energy is tense; rather than connecting, I'm entering with a head of steam to defend my position, guard up. Leveraging empathy, a value we as designers employ consistently in our work, I want to pivot to begin a session with active listening. And I don't just mean nodding my head: absorbing, processing, and probing deeper based on what I'm learning. What was the other group's viewpoint? Where were their tension points coming from?

This would inform the Contextual Micro Exercise, with the goal of reducing friction toward better collaboration. Tracking efficacy on the Progress Card side allows me to note evolution and points of potential pivot each time I have the opportunity to engage.

MMW is robust with a few other complementary processes and artifacts, and I've mostly just scratched the surface here. But what I want you to take away from all of this, agnostic of the platform, is straightforward: whether you're leveraging something like MMW or taking notes on your personal narrative and scratching down your

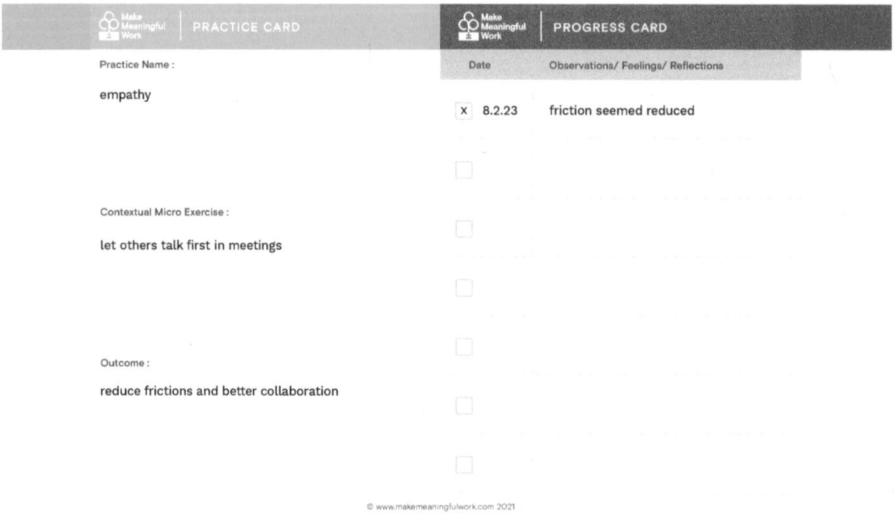

Make Meaningful Work	PRACTICE CARD		Make Meaningful Work	PROGRESS CARD	
Practice Name :			Date	Observations/ Feelings/ Reflections	
empathy			x 8.2.23	friction seemed reduced	
			☐		
Contextual Micro Exercise :			☐		
let others talk first in meetings			☐		
			☐		
Outcome :			☐		
reduce frictions and better collaboration			☐		
			☐		

© www.makemeaningfulwork.com 2021

FIG 1.3: The Practice Card helps us track our progress via real-world dynamics

observed practices in a notebook, you'll ultimately be building a record of what's important to you, how you most successfully engage, and where you're most fulfilled. Coming into this process with a humble mindset toward your evolution best serves its benefit and, most importantly, you.

In fact, when we consider values that are a cornerstone to our journey—truly, the journey of any career path—humility is as essential as it comes. And this is where we'll focus next.

chapter

3

humility: an essen- tial value

Ego cannot exist in any environment where there are experiences to craft, design goals to be achieved, and human beings to engage.

Humility, a designer's essential value—that has a nice ring to it. What about humility, an office manager's essential value? Or a dentist's? Or a librarian's? They all sound great. When humility is our guiding light, the path is always open for fulfillment, evolution, connection, and engagement. In this chapter, we're going to talk about why.

That said, this is a book for designers, and to that end, I'd like to start with a story—well, a journey, really. It's a personal one, and I'm going to make myself a bit vulnerable along the way. I call it:

the tale of justin's preposterous pate

When I was coming out of art school, a long-haired, goateed neophyte, print was a known quantity to me; design on the web, however, was rife with complexities to navigate and discover, a problem to be solved. Though I had been formally trained in graphic design, typography, and layout, what fascinated me was how these traditional skills might be applied to a fledgling digital landscape. This theme would ultimately shape the rest of my career.

So rather than graduate and go into print like many of my friends, I devoured HTML and JavaScript books into the wee hours of the morning and taught myself how to code during my senior year. I wanted—nay, needed—to better understand the underlying implications of what my design decisions would mean once rendered in a browser.

The late '90s and early 2000s were the so-called 'Wild West' of web design. Designers at the time were all figuring out how to apply design and visual communication to the digital landscape. What were the rules? How could we break them and still engage, entertain, and convey information? At a more macro level, how could my values, inclusive of humility, respect, and connection, align in tandem with that? I was hungry to find out.

Though I'm talking about a different era, those are timeless considerations between non-career interactions and the world of design. What are your core passions, or values, that transcend medium? It's essentially the same concept we discussed earlier on the direct parallels between what fulfills you, agnostic of the tangible or digital realms; the core themes are all the same.

First within tables, animated GIFs, Flash, then with Web Standards, divs, and CSS, there was personality, raw unbridled creativity, and unique means of presentment that often defied any semblance of a visible grid. Splash screens and 'browser requirement' pages aplenty. Usability and accessibility were typically victims of such a creation, but such paramount facets of any digital design were largely (and, in hindsight, unfairly) disregarded at the expense of experimentation.

For example, this iteration of my personal portfolio site ('the pseudoroom') from that era was experimental, if not a bit heavy-handed, in the visual communication of the concept of a living sketchbook {FIG 2}. Very skeuomorphic. I collaborated with fellow designer and dear friend Marc Clancy (now a co-founder of the creative project organizing app Milanote) on this one, where we'd first sketch and then pass a Photoshop file back and forth to trick things out and play with varied user interactions. Then, I'd break it down and code it into a digital layout.

Along with design folio pieces, the site also offered free downloads for Mac OS customizations: desktop wallpapers that were effectively design experimentation, custom-designed typefaces, and desktop icons.

From around the same time, GUI Galaxy was a design, pixel art, and Mac-centric news portal some graphic designer friends and I conceived, designed, developed, and deployed {FIG 2.1}.

Design news portals were incredibly popular during this period, featuring (what would now be considered) Tweet-size, small-format snippets of pertinent news from the categories I previously mentioned. If you took Twitter, curated it to a few categories, and wrapped it in a custom-branded experience, you'd have a design news portal from the late 90s / early 2000s.

We as designers had evolved and created a bandwidth-sensitive, web standards award-winning, much more accessibility-conscious website. Still ripe with experimentation, yet more mindful of equitable engagement. You can see a couple of content panes here, noting general news (tech, design) and Mac-centric news below. We also offered many of the custom downloads I cited before as present on my folio site but branded and themed to GUI Galaxy.

The site's backbone was a homegrown CMS, with the presentation layer consisting of global design + illustration + news author collaboration. And the collaboration effort here, in addition to experimentation on a 'brand' and content delivery, was hitting my core. We were designing something bigger than any single one of us and connecting with a global audience.

Collaboration and connection transcend medium in their impact,

FIG 2: "the pseudoroom" website, hitting the sketchbook metaphor hard

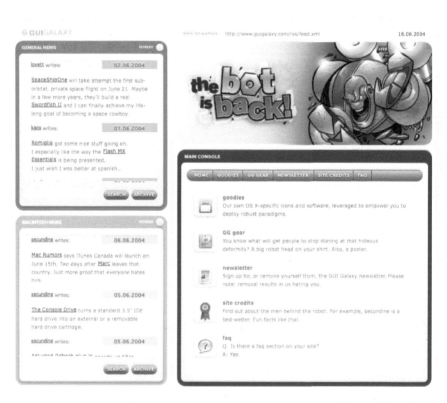

FIG 2.1: GUI Galaxy, web standards-compliant design news portal

immensely fulfilling me as a designer.

Now, why am I taking you down this trip of design memory lane? Two reasons.

First, there's a reason for the nostalgia for that design era (the 'Wild West' era, as I called it earlier): the inherent exploration, personality, and creativity that saturated many design portals and personal portfolio sites. Ultra-finely detailed pixel art UI, custom illustration, bespoke vector graphics, all underpinned by a strong design community.

Today's web design has been in a period of stagnation. I suspect there's a strong chance you've seen a site whose structure looks something like this: a hero image / banner with text overlaid, perhaps with a lovely rotating carousel of images (laying the snark on heavy there), a call to action, and three columns of sub-content directly beneath. Maybe an icon library is employed with selections that vaguely relate to their respective content.

Design, as it's applied to the digital landscape, is in dire need of thoughtful layout, typography, and visual engagement that goes hand-in-hand with all the modern considerations we now know are paramount: usability. Accessibility. Load times and bandwidth-sensitive content delivery. A responsive presentation that meets human beings wherever they're engaging from. We must be mindful of, and respectful toward, those concerns—but not at the expense of creativity of visual communication or via replicating cookie-cutter layouts.

pixel problems

Websites during this period were often designed and built on Macs whose OS and desktops looked something like this. This is Mac OS 7.5, but 8 and 9 weren't that different {FIG 2.2}.

Desktop icons fascinated me: how could any single one, at any given point, stand out to get my attention? In this example, the user's desktop is tidy, but think of a more realistic example with icon pandemonium. Or, say an icon was part of a larger system grouping (fonts, extensions, control panels)—how did it also maintain cohesion amongst a group?

These were 32 x 32 pixel creations, utilizing a 256-color palette, designed pixel-by-pixel as mini mosaics. To me, this was the embodiment of digital visual communication under such ridiculous constraints. And often, ridiculous restrictions can yield the purification of concept and theme.

So I began to research and do my homework. I was a student of this new medium, hungry to dissect, process, discover, and make it my own.

Expanding upon the notion of exploration, I wanted to see how I could push the limits of a 32x32 pixel grid with that 256-color palette. Those ridiculous constraints forced a clarity of concept and presentation that I found incredibly appealing. The digital gauntlet had been tossed, and that challenge fueled me. And so, in my dorm

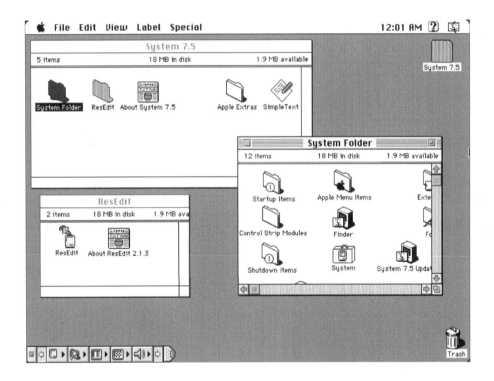

FIG 2.2: A Mac OS 7.5-centric desktop

FIG 2.3: A selection of my pixel art design, 32x32 pixel canvas, 8-bit palette

FIG 2.4: The K10k website

room into the wee hours of the morning, I toiled away, bringing conceptual sketches into mini mosaic fruition.

These are some of my creations, utilizing the only tool available at the time to create icons called ResEdit {FIG 2.3}. ResEdit was a clunky, built-in Mac OS utility not really made for exactly what we were using it for. At the core of all of this work: Research. Challenge. Problem-solving. Again, these core connection-based values are agnostic of medium.

There's one more design portal I want to talk about, which also serves as the second reason for my story to bring this all together.

This is K10k, short for Kaliber 1000. K10k was founded in 1998 by Michael Schmidt and Toke Nygaard, and was **the** design news portal on the web during this period {FIG 2.4}. With its pixel art-fueled presentation, ultra-focused care given to every facet and detail, and with many of the more influential designers of the time who were invited to be news authors on the site, well... it was the place to be, my friend. With respect where respect is due, GUI Galaxy's concept was inspired by what these folks were doing.

For my part, the combination of my web design work and pixel art exploration began to get me some notoriety in the design scene. Eventually, K10k noticed and added me as one of their very select group of news authors to contribute content to the site.

Amongst my personal work and side projects—and now with this inclusion—in the design community, this put me on the map. My design work also began to be published in various printed collections, in magazines domestically and overseas, and featured on other design news portals. With that degree of success while in my early twenties, something else happened:

I evolved—devolved, really—into a colossal asshole (and in just about a year out of art school, no less). The press and the praise became what fulfilled me, and they went straight to my head. They inflated my ego. I actually felt somewhat superior to my fellow designers.

The casualties? My design stagnated. Its evolution—my evolution—stagnated.

I felt so supremely confident in my abilities that I effectively stopped researching and discovering. When previously sketching concepts or iterating ideas in lead was my automatic step one, I instead leaped right into Photoshop. I drew my inspiration from the smallest of sources (and with blinders on). Any critique of my work from my peers was often vehemently dismissed. The most tragic loss: I had lost touch with my values.

My ego almost cost me some of my friendships and burgeoning professional relationships. I was toxic in talking about design and in collaboration. But thankfully, those same friends gave me a priceless gift: candor. They called me out on my unhealthy behavior.

Admittedly, it was a gift I initially did not accept but ultimately was able to deeply reflect upon. I was soon able to accept, and process, and course correct. The realization laid me low, but the re-awakening was essential. I let go of the "reward" of adulation and re-centered upon what stoked the fire for me in art school. Most importantly: I got back to my core values.

always students

Following that short-term regression, I was able to push forward in my personal design and career. And I could self-reflect as I got older to facilitate further growth and course correction as needed.

As an example, let's talk about the Large Hadron Collider. The LHC was designed *"to help answer some of the fundamental open questions in physics, which concern the basic laws governing the interactions and forces among the elementary objects, the deep structure of space and time, and in particular the interrelation between quantum mechanics and general relativity."* Thanks, Wikipedia.

Around fifteen years ago, in one of my earlier professional roles, I designed the interface for the application that generated the LHC's particle collision diagrams. These diagrams are the rendering of what's actually happening inside the Collider during any given particle collision event and are often considered works of art unto themselves.

Designing the interface for this application was a fascinating process for me, in that I worked with Fermilab physicists to understand what the application was trying to achieve, but also how the physicists themselves would be using it. To that end, in this role, I cut my teeth on usability testing, working with the Fermilab team to iterate and improve the interface. How they spoke and what they spoke about was like an alien language to me. And by making myself humble and working under the mindset that I was but a student, I made myself available to be a part of their world to generate that vital connection.

I also had my first ethnographic observation experience: going to the Fermilab location and observing how the physicists used the tool in their actual environment, on their actual terminals. For example, one takeaway was that due to the level of ambient light-driven contrast within the facility, the data columns ended up using white text on a dark gray background instead of black text-on-white. This enabled them to pore over reams of data during the day and ease their eye strain. And Fermilab and CERN are government entities with rigorous accessibility standards, so my knowledge in that realm also grew. The barrier-free design was another essential form of connection.

So to those core drivers of my visual problem-solving soul and ultimate fulfillment: discovery, exposure to new media, observation, human connection, and evolution. What opened the door for those values was me checking my ego before I walked through it.

An evergreen willingness to listen, learn, understand, grow, evolve, and connect yields our best work. In particular, I want to focus on the words 'grow' and 'evolve' in that statement. If we are always students of our craft, we are also continually making ourselves available to evolve. Yes, we have years of applicable design study under our belt. Or the focused lab sessions from a UX bootcamp. Or the monogrammed portfolio of our work. Or, ultimately, decades of a career behind us.

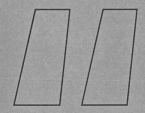

An evergreen willingness to listen, learn, understand, grow, evolve, and connect yields our best work. If we are always students of our craft, we are also continually making ourselves available to evolve.

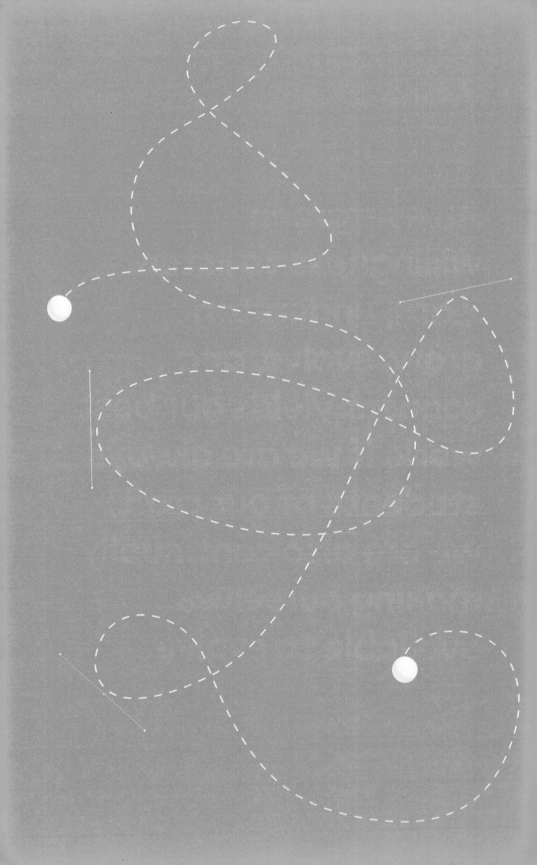

But all that said: experience does not equal 'expert.'

As soon as we close our minds via an inner monologue of 'knowing it all' or branding ourselves a '#thoughtleader' on social media, the designer we **are** is our final form. The designer we **can be** will never exist.

propelling our team interactions

Humility is also essential to how designers create together as a team.

Ego cannot exist in any environment where there are experiences to craft, design goals to be achieved, and human beings to engage. It puts blinders on toward an objective approach, a me-over-we mindset taking precedence over an inclusive process. The potential variables at play here—UX, visual communication, usability, accessibility—should have no degree of subjectivity in their DNA.

In fact, subjectivity is poison to the design process: in feedback, in decision-making, in creative direction, feature prioritization, etc. Evolution, quality, experience, and engagement are all on the line when ego and whim lead. And this notion of subjectivity versus objectivity translates directly to how we give feedback: what is actionable, and what is articulated from the hip?

For example, on feedback specifically:

Subjective approach: *I like it!*

- This is 'nice' to hear. It can be affirming or feel good. But what then, after the hit of dopamine? How can I leverage 'I like it' moving forward?I made a decision on my direction (personally, by my work, with the company).

Objective approach: *This is successful because [x]. Or, This aligns to project goals (or test results, or data) because of [y].*
- 'Successful' ties feedback to supporting points of project goals that confirm why the given approach works. Less *"I like it because it's blue"* and more *"I appreciate how you integrated blue as the primary call to action color amongst the rest of the client's brand palette; it draws a user's eye to areas of action organically."*

And on the other side of the coin:

Subjective approach: *That sucks.*
- A bit of an extreme example, but the point is that feedback that is a variant of "Eh" or "I don't really like it" yields zero growth for the recipient.

Objective approach: *This doesn't achieve user (or project, or business, or environment) goals because [z].*
- This is the feedback that is conducive to evolution; in both my work, as well as my tactics and strategy. If I can see where my design isn't aligning with foundational research and learning, there's growth to

be had. Less *"I don't like it because it's blue,"* and more *"we learned from our accessibility testing that reversed white text on the blue tone you're using doesn't pass WCAG AA standards. Have you explored other options?"*

Design isn't 'good' or 'bad'—those are subjective terms (sorry, Dieter). Design is aligned to goals, and its efficacy is determined from their attainment or otherwise. 'Successful' or 'unsuccessful' are more apt descriptors, and that directly frames how we should give feedback in kind.

And let's be real—we're all friends here—being in receipt of any feedback, even if it's the most goal-focused, objective-based, humbly delivered feedback, can sometimes be challenging to digest or 'entertain,' let's say. When you're advocating for humans in design, or advocating for connection, or heck just for what you think is most successful, design can be personal (because you made it). You poured yourself into it. Even when it's created at a product, enterprise level, or data-informed capacity.

Just to be clear, I'm not saying don't defend your work or thought process—not by a long shot. I am saying make yourself present and available to the receipt of objective feedback. That's what it's all about. Evolution begets connection, and connection begets fulfillment.

As I wrote in *Creative Culture*:

When we make ourselves openly available to constructive feedback, we are doing our part to contribute to the ultimate betterment of a piece of work. By checking our egos at the door, we're innately operating in unison, instead of hierarchical cliques.

I cannot say this more emphatically: It's good to be humbled. Being surrounded by incredible talent and immersed in the brilliance of your team is a distinct gift, not a check on your own self-esteem.

No matter how much knowledge we have accrued and our depth of experience over various projects, we cannot impose a solution simply because we feel it's correct. We test, we refine, we test again, all aimed at creating an organically perfected user experience.

As passionate craftspeople, we can guide and advise, being cognizant of how the user will best achieve their goals. Doing so makes for better design. It's no ding in our fender to iterate, learn, and evolve. Just as we accept this fact—metaphorically stepping aside to allow user empathy and connection to guide us—we must do the same for the skill sets and abilities of our team members.

What we find all too often in any business setting where designers exist is that stakeholders at the team level, or higher in the seniority chain, can (and do) impose constraints throughout the process. Be it from a project's inception, or throughout its entire lifecycle. When there is too much ego in the room, there isn't much space left

Design isn't 'good' or 'bad'—those are subjective terms. Design is aligned to goals, and its efficacy is determined from their attainment or otherwise.

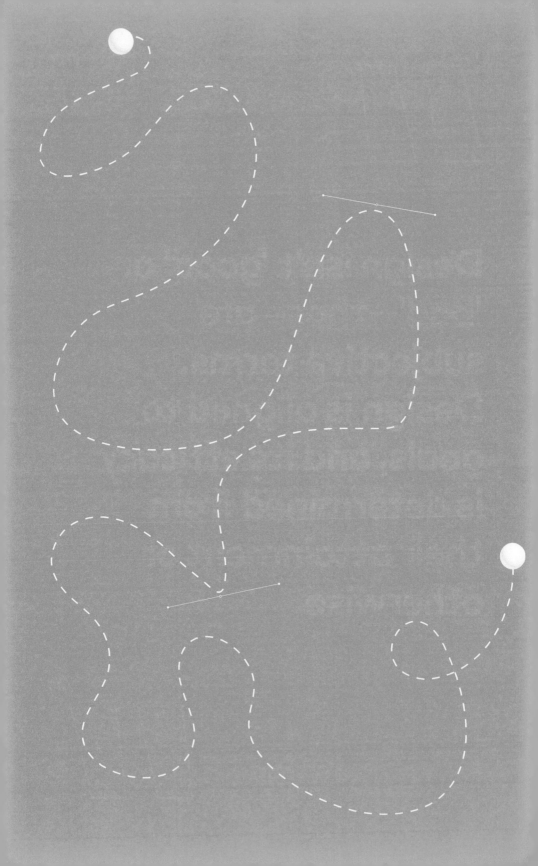

for creative pursuit.

To be humble is to be respectful of your work, of those who will be engaging with your work, and of the bigger picture of its impact on the community and environment. Really, so many of those values we as designers employ in our work (humility and respect cited here, but also empathy, compassion, connection, engagement) are also directly applicable to what comprises a healthy work culture—**where** you work.

To be fulfilled and do our best work, there must be a symbiosis at play, one that exists between the environment that surrounds us in person or remotely and what we, as designers, put back into it.

chapter

4

# of culture and craft

A healthy culture is designed to be that way. It strives to connect us to one another—and to our collaborative work—agnostic of a remote or in-person seat.

THE GIRLFRIENDS
THE SPICERS
KATE + BOB
ROY-BROOKS HEINECK 10-11-13
SEP 1990
Carol + Chris 8-17-2012
VICKI
R♥R
John
PLOT THICK
MILLERS 200
Rachel

"You could've probably written a couple of books or different book topics being a designer … What made you decide to write a book on this topic: culture in a creative environment?"

That was the question posed to me on "What is UX," the podcast of design agency Impekable founder Pek Pongpaet. We were discussing the impetus for Creative Culture, and my answer boiled down to this: in order to do our best work, the environment where we create must echo the same values as the process of how we create. An inclusive, people-first culture has to have a direct parallel to an inclusive, people-first design process.

A business can't claim to be 'people-first' and not have demonstrative practices in place in hiring, org culture, diversity, remote work support, design process, product ethics, or environmental impact. Any one facet of support isn't a validation of that claim; it's a farce. Too many organizations miss that mark, hence the purpose behind that first book—I had some thoughts on the matter.

To that end, let's focus on 'the environment where we create.' Dan Szuc cites the imperative harmony between where and how we're creating:

"Work is an environment and this includes people's work places, spaces, offices and cultures. Projects exist in this environment. You can intentionally play a role that has a positive or negative effect on that environment. When examining a project's environment, there are two sides to consider. It is critical that both sides integrate with one another to create environments that allow meaningful work, as follows:

1. Process side - this helps you to deliver and usually consists of such things as project plans, people, disciplines, process, methods, methodologies; and gaining a sense of direction through vision, mission and values.

2. Culture side - this involves having an intentional, explicit focus on the interaction and relationships between people and practices that help a project not only to perform and deliver but also to create a place where people actually thrive in making together.

These two sides must both be present and work in tandem. Consider the duality and multi-threaded practices that exist on both sides in a connected fashion."

Let's put a critical eye on what comprises such an environment and precisely how it drives connection.

what makes for a culture of fulfillment?

To answer this question, let's start with what doesn't. In the first story of this book, I planted a seed that I intended to come back and harvest:

"After a year or so in this position, the tradeoff of doing unfulfilling work began to take its toll on me and my design. The cultural issues that were prevalent on my team weren't helping."

There can be a difference between a manager and a leader; they're not always synonyms. 'Manager' is a job title, a parking spot or a business card payoff. Show me an unsupported team, and I'll show you a manager who defines themself by their LinkedIn heading over their service.

Anyone can be a leader, regardless of position on an org chart, experience, title, or tenure. Demonstrative respect, initiative, care, compassion, and support are some of the hallmarks of someone who excels in that capacity. When an organization is headed by business card titles—or a team managed by a LinkedIn heading—there are foundational cracks in the culture from the top down created by that leadership void.

In this book's introductory story, I had a business card title-caliber manager. The lack of fulfillment from my design work was well-complemented by their complete disinterest in leading or supporting team dynamics. Lack of accountability saturated our interactions, and being thrown under the bus was uncommon. As one of a handful of friends who founded the company—now in an executive-level position by default—this behavior was not only tolerated but was in the DNA of the company's culture (recall the Ben & Jerry's story from Chapter 2).

Bad managers are but one symptom of a culture that can inhibit our growth. We've gone from macro to micro in other examples: from ethics misalignment to the impact of ego, down to the delivery of subjective feedback. Are employees respectfully treated as unique individuals with unique voices or as unknown names on an

Excel spreadsheet? Is 'unlimited vacation' a perk that's actually impossible to leverage in practice due to mismanaged workloads and expectations? Or are people actually able to rest and recalibrate as they need?

In some capacity, on some variation of those themes, most of us have likely been impacted by similar unhealthy practices.

ok, but what makes for a culture of fulfillment?

The same values in the DNA of a healthy culture—compassion, humility, inclusion, and respect among them—must also be intrinsic in the organization's design process. For us to be most fulfilled in what we create, the culture around us must drive the same connection in how we create. Else, the disconnection between incongruous values in action makes for disconnection in totality: us to ourselves, us to our work, our teams, and on and on.

A culture of fulfillment is a planned, living, and nourished ecosystem of support and engagement that facilitates success. It doesn't exist by chance and isn't simply sustained by the light of its own virtue. A healthy culture is **designed** to be that way. It strives to connect us to one another—and to our collaborative work—agnostic of a remote or in-person seat. And its values are harmonious with our own, fueling an ethical symbiosis devoid of internal conflict.

The concept of care and feeding given to a piece of work we

produce, from sketch to release to iteration and beyond, is imperative for sustaining a healthy culture. To find a culture of fulfillment is to find a healthy environment that's championed and supported from the top down—either in an executive-level role specifically dedicated to this purpose or through empowered managers who embody and champion the business' values.

finding your cultural fit to do your best work

Like the term 'framework,' 'culture fit' can be a swear word—particularly when a business uses the term outwardly toward job candidates to perpetuate bias.

However, from job seeker to business, 'culture fit' is a valid concept. Not everyone can (or wants to) be a part of an environment where work/life balance is compromised at the expense of 'comfort in ambiguity'—another job description term that's often code for "we don't have our shit together as an organization." If that doesn't outwardly seem like a place where you could do your best work, your fit to that business' culture would not be there.

Identifying and prioritizing the values we covered earlier—and noting where you're most fulfilled—will be invaluable in this process.

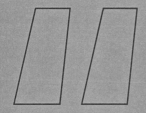

A culture of fulfillment is a planned, living, and nourished ecosystem of support and engagement that facilitates success. It doesn't exist by chance and isn't simply sustained by the light of its own virtue.

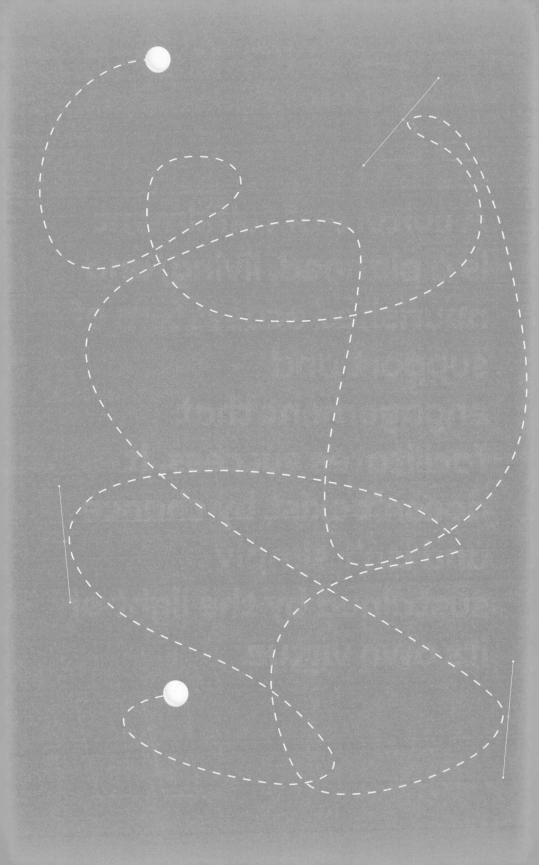

Having that knowledge at the ready, you'll be able to ascertain where a potential employer aligns with your most essential needs versus what you might have to experience in a diminished capacity (or not at all).

As noted by Harvard Business Review, *"In ADP Research Institute's most recent 50,000-person surveys of stratified random samples of working populations around the world, the most powerful predictors of retention, performance, engagement, resilience, and inclusion did not include pay or liking one's colleagues or work location or even a strong belief in the mission of the organization."*

None of those netted out as significantly as these three points:

1. Was I excited to work every day last week?
2. Did I have a chance to use my strengths every day?
3. At work do I get an opportunity to do what I'm good at and something I love?

In short: *"Was I fulfilled by what, and where, I created?"*

Given that an environment with the systems in place for you to evolve, thrive, and succeed is imperative toward your connection and fulfillment, being able to look for its healthy signs is a key skill. With work increasingly widely distributed across remote, hybrid, or in-person engagements, those signs can be nuanced and environment-specific. From a company's website to a posted job description to the dialogue of the job interview, a composite picture of the company's values will start to take shape. What is said and shown is just as telling as what isn't.

For example, in *Creative Culture* I wrote:

"Identify some companies you would love to work with and begin to investigate their story and the way they tell it. How do you feel they portray themselves? What seems most important to them? How do they speak about their people and their work? Which of those (people, or work) have preferential hierarchy in the navigation on their website?"

Just like in client work, when undertaking an internal website design a business goes through an information architecture process, prioritizing content and the hierarchy of sections within the site navigation. In practice, they're showing their hand about what they value most. Where is something like 'Our People' placed (or is it placed at all?) versus 'Our Executive Board'? Is there 'day in the life'-caliber content present on the site? If present, does it describe an environment where you feel you can thrive? Has the content been updated to reflect remote or hybrid working?

What does their content portray on their 'About Us' page? Does it represent those doing the work within the organization, or the C-Suite exclusively? If both are present, who is listed first? If there is an executive board within the organization, is it a diverse ensemble? The answers to these questions can give you a sense of potential alignment with this business, or otherwise, before you click 'apply now' on their relevant job posting(s).

an eye on the content

If you don't have an 'in' at a company or aren't referred in some capacity, one of two scenarios will likely occur as it pertains to viewing a job posting: either you'll come across a post on a job listing website that seems intriguing enough to do research on the business, or you'll do research on an intriguing company and perhaps find a fit on their Careers page. Whatever the sequence, how that post is written is another huge 'tell' about their priorities and how they may align with your own.

We've already covered a few red flags to watch out for, like unlimited vacation and 'comfort in ambiguity.' The former is often unattainable in any capacity as the support systems around 'unlimited vacation' are never put in place—peer pressure, lack of managerial support, or consistently unrealistic expectations around workload and delivery are omnipresent blockers. The latter intimates a culture of disorganization and immaturity, and it's not the only phrase that gives it away.

Without healthy boundaries, a business will consume as much of you as you're open to giving. Many organizations wear their burnout culture on their sleeve in how they articulate their expectations in a job posting: 'Overachievers Wanted' is a headline I saw within the hour of writing this section. Is their environment 'fast-paced'? Are you expected to be a 'self-starter'? These descriptors are the real estate ad equivalent of qualifying a small living space as 'cozy' or a home needing ample repair with 'great potential.' They're all explicitly chosen marketing-speak phrases with an underlying meaning about what you're in for, should you commit.

   As I noted earlier, we also need to identify the unseen: what is said and shown is just as telling as what isn't. Fulfillment is essential, but being compensated for what you bring to the table is equally imperative. To that end, is salary information included in the post? If not...why not? To compensate fairly is to be respectful, and omission or vague language (for example, the dreaded 'commensurate with experience') is a window into how the organization values its employees.

the other eye on the process

Let's say you've found an organization that seems like a good fit, have reached out to express your interest, and end up hearing back from them. Fantastic! This marks a seminal point of observation to take note of their values in action throughout the interview process—from that initial outreach to scheduling to the 'at the table' conversation in and of itself.

As I noted earlier, we also need to identify the unseen: what is said and shown is just as telling as what isn't. Fulfillment is essential, but being compensated for what you bring to the table is equally imperative. To that end, is salary information included in the post? If not...why not? To compensate fairly is to be respectful, and omission or vague language (for example, the dreaded 'commensurate with experience') is a window into how the organization values its employees.

We know how values misalignment can ultimately come back to haunt us, so ensuring harmony with your own is vital at this nascent stage. Consider the scheduling process in and of itself: sometimes you're dealing with a hiring manager, sometimes HR, or sometimes the person you'd be reporting to.

There was a time, pre-COVID-19 pandemic, during my tenure as the VP of Design at a healthcare technology company when I was reaching out to candidates directly to schedule in-person conversations. One such dialogue I hoped to have was aligned with a job posting that went up in February. Now, Chicago is known for its extremes in weather at both ends of the spectrum: often uncomfortably warm summers and brutally cold and snowy winters. This February was true to frigid form.

The candidate and I connected and set up a day and time for them to come in for a chat. The day before we were set to meet, a massive snowstorm was set to roll in, hitting the city overnight. This would undoubtedly wreak havoc with the following morning's commute.

Having had the misfortune of making my way to an interview during severe weather in the past—or hell, having had to head to bed the preceding evening stressed out if a threatened storm might make things more complex—I tried to put myself in this person's shoes.

I reached out and offered to reschedule our conversation, given the potential weather complications. The candidate expressed tremendous relief, noting they'd be coming into the city from the suburbs and were planning for the worst. We selected a new date and time free from Jack Frost's ire.

Before a person applying for a role is an applicant, they're a human being. Values in action at this stage—empathy, compassion, respect, in this instance—demonstrated to them who we were as a business, as a team, and for me personally, as a potential manager.

Once you're through a values-aligned scheduling process and at the conversation stage, have questions at the ready that drive at the core of what is most important to you and your success. For example, as it applies to remote work:

- How are you supporting connections among teammates?
- Do you work asynchronously as a team?
- What are your core meeting hours?
- How are your business' values translated to remote interactions?

Remember: this is a mutual interview. You're gauging whether this organization, this team, and these people are part of an environment where you'll be supported to do your best, most fulfilling work. The responses you receive, and the process leading up to having this dialogue, will be strong signs of their ultimate fit for you.

the means to make your most meaningful work

Consider what we discussed in Chapter 2: through the lens of the MMW platform, we went through a process of identifying the practices where we thrive, noting how they drive connection to our environment, one another, and our work. In turn, this connection helps fuel a culture where we're functioning to our utmost potential in actions over words.

As I wrote earlier in this section: *"A healthy culture is designed to be that way."* Of course, a massive part of this intention is how an organization—and those it empowers—drives culture from the top down, leading by example: How values are tangibly demonstrated. How employees are respected, supported, and viewed as more than names on a spreadsheet ('resources'). How the work, and those who will engage with it, aren't victims of release cadence or senior stakeholder whim. And from within, what outcomes from the work are ultimately celebrated?

Another side of that intention is leveraging the values we as designers preach in our process—empathy, compassion, inclusion, respect—back into how we engage with our co-workers and teammates. When there is harmony between practice and process, the groundwork for being fulfilled by what, and where, we create is laid.

designing the culture around you

"Designers and front-enders have a unique advantage at solving the cultural problems that are sucking the life out of us."

The above quote from *Creative Culture* (that should've cited much broader disciplines, in hindsight) refers to the values that must already be employed in our work, given their connection with other living beings: compassion, empathy, respect, humility. Because we need to incorporate those values in the creation process, we have a constant connection-centric mindset to draw from in our environment.

When that recognition is combined with the power of our own identified values, the potential of what we're able to put back into our environment to drive connection and fulfillment is massively amplified.

Consider some 'standard' day-to-day interactions we may encounter (teams-to-teams, teammates-to-teammates, teammates to their work):

- Writing asynchronous messages
- Giving feedback in design reviews (a favorite topic of mine, clearly)
- Sending meeting invites

Where are the points of opportunity in the above to engage respectfully and craft an environment of connection?

Meeting/calendar invites can come in a variety of flavors: 1:1's. Project kick-offs. Stand-ups. Regroups. Post-mortems...you get the point. And very often, when you're sending out a meeting invite, finding time on someone's calendar (or multiple people's calendars) can be very challenging.

But then—look at that! {FIG 3} What's this? Is that a mirage? The noon-to-one o'clock block on this person's calendar always seems to be open. This is a moment of decision: *"This time is available, but should I take it?"* Ultimately, this is like when you're looking for a parking spot and wonder how everyone missed that perfect spot— which ends up being where a fire hydrant is. It's open for a reason.

People leave this open because, believe it or not, they'd like to decompress. That decompression typically manifests itself in what we call 'lunch.' Pausing with intent. Taking time to refuel. Or, it could be time to connect with coworkers. Or go for a walk. Or plainly do whatever they want. It's their right—it's a **human** right.

Respecting this boundary is to be compassionate: recognizing your coworker's lunchtime and not consuming it with a whiteboarding session, retrospective, or design review. This mindset should be

FIG 3: A calendar view of availability—that noon block looks tempting...

standard for us, as designers—compassion in how we create, what we're creating, and how we treat one another as human beings. This is a baseline for designing a culture of fulfillment; we need to go deeper than that.

'Not taking someone's lunchtime' through leveraging compassion is Step One. Let's say that through an MMW Practice Spotting™ exercise you've identified "to connect, begin with action" (referencing my earlier narrative) as a practice where you thrive. Step Two, then, is reaching out to the person to set their expectations on what the discussion is about, what its outcomes would be, and finding a time that best suits them. To that end, you're leveraging a fulfilling practice to build a connection with a teammate who can also be more charged by the culture you're helping to develop, in kind.

This is mindful action with a positive intent toward achieving a specific outcome (connection). **This is design.**

At the individual and team levels, we can craft and leverage rituals built around practices that align with our fulfillment. These rituals can vary in levels of 'formality' or time investment, but their value should never come into question. This time should be consistent and cherished (from a calendar perspective).

How much you get out of a ritual is determined mainly by how it's mindfully designed in advance—what are its requirements, outputs, or desired goals and outcomes? And how do all of these facets align with what's fulfilling for the participants?

One ritual I'm extremely protective of, and value immensely, is the coffee chat. For me, it's as much about enjoying a good cup as it is about slowing down—pausing with intent—to (re)connect and recalibrate. The dynamic imposes a forced context and energy switch: from meetings, presentations, and artifact production to slower-paced conversation and dialogue without pretense. The energy switching can be further augmented by going to a café, either with a coworker in person or having a virtual cup with them via your phone or laptop. The intent there being to physically get out of your home, office, or workspace. Fresh vibe, fresh eyes, fresh mind.

Even a ritual as modest as 'having a coffee with someone' is designed. In this case, the gathering is intentionally small, and the topics are undefined. Malleable, by intent. It's not to say we need to get uncomfortably deep on the subject matter; quite the opposite. A desired outcome is building empathy for a teammate through active listening. Whatever the fine points of the plan, the connection-based yield is tremendous all the same.

On a regular cadence, some rituals can, of course, be more inclusive of time allotment. Consider a weekly session where teammates share their project work, challenges, and accomplishments. Or, agnostic of the medium, sharing what's inspired everyone away from the office the preceding week. Gaining a greater understanding of what fuels one another, together with seeing your teammates as more than an email address, are some goals—better connection and collaboration are targeted outcomes.

Being mindful about the rituals we craft removes the *"why didn't that work?"* -caliber questions from throwing things at the cultural wall to see what sticks. Many of these Band-Aid solutions come from the top down, and aren't so much fulfilling as they are an employee needs-based mismatch:

> *"Remote team members are connection-starved? Let's put copious video happy hours on their calendars—but not during business hours."*

> *"Employees in the office are consistently working inhumane hours week over week? Let's put some pinball machines in the lounge to help them unwind."*

Things that seem 'cool' to someone who has elevated hierarchy on an org chart but haven't been given much thought than *"here you go, have fun"* are where frustration and disconnection amongst employees occur. As designers ascend the ranks, having a profound impact on what drives their teammates' connection, evolution, and success is an incredible opportunity—and a core driver of their own fulfillment.

in leader-
ship

All that said, coasting is not an
option for us. Not as a team
member, not as an independent
contributor, and beyond a doubt,
not in a leadership position.

Over time, you may take some distinct paths in your career as a designer: you'll continue to be close to the craft, the process, and the output, evolving through the continued challenges in creation and the honing of your abilities. Or perhaps you'll find your fulfillment is derived from helping others grow in that capacity, supporting them to achieve their goals, and providing the environment for them to do their best creative work. There's also a less common 'player / coach' route that dips into individual contributor and management spheres, with inherent added complexities. More on that in a moment.

To be clear: there is no 'right' or 'wrong' path here. There's only the recognition of where you best align to continue to drive connection.

There's a mindset that career progression needs to be defined in a way that maps to LinkedIn status updates: junior to mid, mid to senior, senior to director, director to VP, and so on. Some can be so focused on title advancement and rapid echelon climbing that the groundwork of where fulfillment (and values alignment, and ultimately connection) is derived is never understood. We've discussed those perils.

An Art Director within a design organization I previously led has been illustrating, storyboarding, and defining the creative vision for over thirty years. He is one of the most brilliantly talented and experienced people I've ever had the opportunity to collaborate with; he has no want, or need, to manage people—it's all about the craft. Setting the tone. Pushing himself in various media. Helping others achieve growth through inspiration and feedback, not the direct management of them. For him, that's enough; it's everything.

We've covered how—and why—to connect to ourselves, one another, our work, and those who engage with it. That's one path. Leadership, as it pertains to championing design within an organization or supporting those you manage in the craft, is where we'll be focusing.

from 'me' to 'we'

The organizational transition into the direct management of people, a team, or an organization, is different for everyone. The psychological transition is equally bespoke. And mine was challenging on a few levels.

In the introductory story to this book, I recounted that when I became the Lead Interface Designer at that organization I was also tasked with building out a team despite having never managed anyone before. Given how fast the turn was in which I was put into this role, I was unprepared for the potential consequences of immediate people management—though in hindsight, in some capacity, I should have been. I was still relatively new in my career, so it was a distinct challenge, not only because I was now responsible for someone's growth and success beyond my own, but I was also expected to continue to design.

This is the player / coach model I mentioned earlier: personal output on equal footing with people management. Experience in each part of this role is massively helpful to be successful toward the whole responsibility. Though gaining confidence as a designer with healthy momentum, I could've used substantially more coaching on people management in tandem.

Even when folks have significantly more experience than I did then, success in this role can be a non-trivial feat, especially when personal contribution and team support have priorities that can often be at odds with one another. I started to get the hang of things but still found the dynamic complex to navigate. That said, a spark had been lit; helping others achieve their goals planted a seed of fulfillment toward something in me I didn't know existed.

It'd be another handful of years before I'd be in a management position again, and my sense of reward—largely, my identity—had still primarily come from the reception of my design work to this point. The distinct guardrails of this next management role—responsibility for leading, supporting, and growing a team from the ground up—helped give focus to where my fulfillment would need to shift to be successful. Without having the 'player' part of the 'player / coach' dynamic as part of the mix like I did in via that first foray into management, it was also a time to genuinely ask myself: was this the right fit for me?

The answer to that question is unique for everyone. For my part, I aligned my core values—connection, respect, and humility—to how I could champion my team's success and shifted 'hands-on design' rewards over to personal outlets and projects. Once I began translating values to actions, I recognized the answer for me was a resounding 'yes.' This represented a 'from me to we' -caliber shift in mindset and reward: less centering on myself and more on the success of the collective.

Of course, having a clear sense of my values was a tremendous boon toward that clarity and informed how I'd build a culture of support. As a leverageable baseline, this is where Practice Spotting™ is invaluable. Let's see how this plays out via a 161-character micro story and a lean Practice Spotting™ exercise:

> *On a new team member's first day—in person or remote—I'm there to greet them. At the front door if at the office, or via a morning video call welcome if remote.*

I don't have a meeting on my calendar; I've blocked off this time. I'm not distracted by my phone; my focus is on where I need to be and why. My butt is out of my chair, and I'm fully present, literally and metaphorically.

Let's pick out the Explicit Practices for this scenario:

- I set aside time on my calendar
- I get out of my chair
- I meet my new team member at the door

Next, the Implicit Practices behind the tangible actions:

- To connect, begin with action: *I want to show my appreciation for this individual joining my team and the organization, so I make a point to show that by greeting them myself.*
- Looking at the bigger picture: *an employee's first day is the most significant opportunity in the world to show my / our values in demonstrable action.*

- Setting boundaries: *protecting my calendar/schedule to keep this time sacred.*
- Reflection: *I've been in this situation as a new employee before, and feeling disconnected at the point of joining a new organization on my first day.*

And lastly, let's go deeper by breaking down one of those implicit practices, 'to connect, begin with action,' in this case:

Enablers
- A desire to connect
- Empathy
- A sense of responsibility
- Respect

Barriers
- Potential distractions
  - My phone
  - Co-worker conversations
  - The world at large
- Business needs

By looking at the Enablers behind that Implicit Practice, the values in action are crystal clear: connection, empathy, respect. They form the underpinnings of a culture where an employee is appreciated and supported to thrive. In this way, for the team and me: it's ultimately an **environment** of fulfillment on all fronts.

practically speaking

Organizational / cross-department politics, internal / external design education, advocacy, stakeholder management—there's a lot in play that design leaders must navigate (this is where a program like Make Meaningful Work at scale can be invaluable). Providing support and fostering an environment of fulfillment for our teams must be a constant amongst the tumult, and the needle can be consistently moved in practical ways.

I can think of a couple of examples where I've needed to adjust corporate environmental expectations to better demonstrate my team's values and needs. The secret sauce toward making change is aligning results to metrics that are equally advantageous to the business. For example:

At the healthcare company where I was a VP of Design, we'd inherited many of the larger parent company's dashboards, policies, and procedures. Onboarding new employees on a Monday and putting them into a week's worth of corporate training was the standard process. If you recall back in Chapter 2, welcoming new team members on a Friday and doing things decidedly less training-y is much more my bag. So how do we reconcile two very different approaches?

I had a conversation with my boss about The New Day One as I'd leveraged it in a previous role over almost five years—the process and requirements, the human/business value, and ultimately the metrics I'd used to track its efficacy:

- Level of investment (attrition)
  - Compared to the rest of the organization
  - Compared to industry-wide
- Social media mentions (organic marketing)
- Incoming mentions of The New Day one in candidate interviews (organic marketing)

My proposal was this: *"Let's try it out."* Between the two of us, the trust was there to implement without much friction. At the broader organizational level, where the standard operating procedure was a bit different, we also had a foundation of business value-based metrics to implement this change if / when questioned.

In another instance, I was leading the design team within a very utilization culture-driven agency. An employee's utilization percentage was their primary defining metric, so high allocation toward billable work ruled the roost (spoiler: this is the real-world case for the Practice Card example I cited in Chapter 2).

My team members had a standing meeting with some folks within the Account Management organization (those who managed the client relationships), as it pertained to a client they were all engaged with. The designers and researchers would provide updates on the execution front and Account on the relationship front. However, it was a known quantity that this meeting was politically fraught: people butting heads, a lack of listening, participants being on edge. There was such a high amount of anxiety from my team going into these meetings, and negative energy coming out of them, that the subsequent time preceding and following the sessions was more or less a wash on the billable time front.

Now, I'd written quite a bit in *Creative Culture* about how an employee's value cannot be defined by their billability; that's Corporate Dehumanization 101. For my team, these meetings' outcomes largely involved distraction and challenge in getting refocused back to their work. To make change that mattered, we needed to employ a shift that would go counter to the overall hyper utilization model and was compassionately human-driven, with a complement of business value to facilitate the change needed.

For the next standing meeting, I asked the team to **not** put time toward client work the hour preceding that session. Close the laptop. Read a book, go for a walk, or take a power nap. This would produce a different kind of energy in advance—one of calm—and would comprise the first adjustment of three:

1. Pause with intent
2. Employ active listening

3. Leverage our values (empathy, compassion)

Rather than meeting the politically fraught energy brought into the space, we employed active listening (not just head nodding and silence, per se, but follow-up questions. Observation. Visual and verbal cues). We also leveraged our values of compassion and empathy in our work in a foundational sense: let's bring those same values into the session. The energy the other team was bringing into the room was perhaps rolling downhill from the client. Account was the frontline of communication, after all.

For that next meeting, rather than two bulls charging at one another and interlocking horns, the energy from the other team wasn't met; it was defused. We listened, observed, questioned, and led by engaging them as human beings. The lenses they brought to the table, their challenges and their energy's impetus, were revealed.

Subsequent meetings further built bridges and increased communication. One unbilled hour yielded hours saved on the backend: quicker time to refocus saved floundering cycles post-meeting. Enhanced collaboration and communication reduced versioning. Having this metric in my back pocket was a direct point of value to further demonstrate the perils of hyper-utilization focus for further necessary change—slowing down to speed up.

the dangers of coasting

The COVID-19 pandemic has forced us to continually reevaluate ways to healthily stay connected. Let's pause to think about what we've collectively faced as leaders, nay human beings, over this time and in what is now the new normal. Over the flux, stress, and uncertainty, ensuring our teams have been as connected and fulfilled remotely as they were in person has been a fluid and evolving challenge.

We've needed to:

- Adapt our working style and how we support our teams
- Ensure they're fulfilled by their work and connected to one another
- Humbly listen, respond, and adjust to their feedback

And what are some things that we've tried along the way? At the onset, I thought: *"let's try a shift to copious video meetings so the team can maintain some face time,"* which ultimately led to too many video sessions and overall video fatigue.

Okay then, how about video happy hours so we can decompress as a team outside the context of deliverables? Yeah, this also led to too many video sessions and overall video fatigue.

Pivoting from there (*"enough video already,"* was the paraphrased takeaway) to align to supporting asynchronous working and message checking as primary processes worked quite well as demonstrative methods of respect. Re-setting expectations on meeting hours and potential attendance was an organic procedural transition.

But inclusive of these connection-based adaptive efforts, it's still an evolving challenge, right?

In fact, according to a recent Pew Research study, via the pandemic and the shift to flexible work dynamics, 65% of workers still say they feel less connected to their coworkers. There have been mass amounts of attrition agnostic of industry over this time, making it even more challenging to maintain team health when so many people are testing the market.

In short, we've been in a consistent position of helping our teams navigate extreme change while we ourselves navigate radical change. But what we find is that when we're focusing on the well-being of others, we can forget to turn that same compassionate lens inward: what of the connection with ourselves, in kind? Where do we ensure our own fulfillment, best aligning our values to our livelihoods?

I've had a few distinct moments in my career in design leadership where I've recognized my disconnection. With that understanding comes two options: assess where the detachment lies and realign to my values, or accept that the gulf is too deep and will hinder me from best supporting my team.

In one instance, I had a Roy Scheider in *Jaws*-caliber dolly zoom moment during a design review—this was in my Director of Design days in the agency world. The problem-solving, the design process, the incredible team: all aspects of the environment I was charged by. We

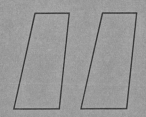

What we find is that when we're focusing on the well-being of others, we can forget to turn that same compassionate lens inward: what of the connection with ourselves, in kind?

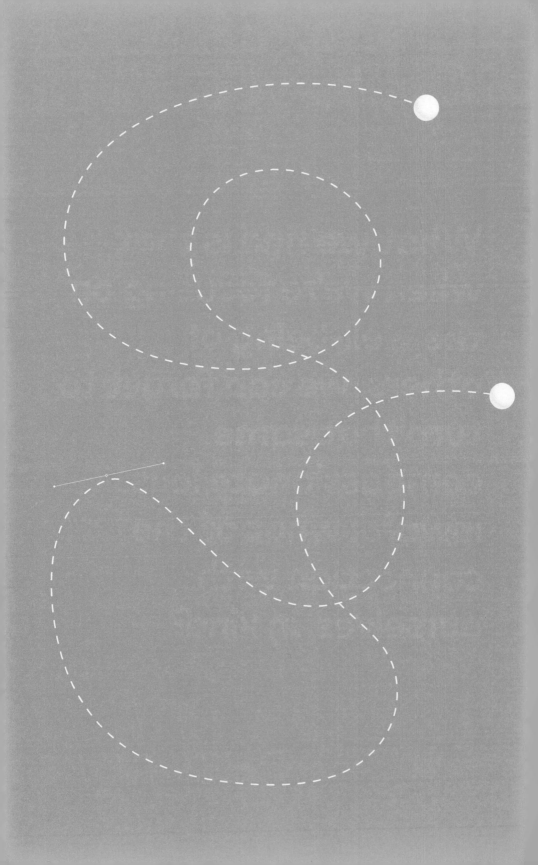

had some very cool clients across a variety of markets, but in the cited point of clarity I realized that I was no longer connected with them or the work. Agency engagements were no longer fulfilling a need within me: the application of design toward a sector in which I could leverage it to actually try to help people in need.

My disconnection left a sick feeling in the pit of my stomach, as I knew it was unacceptable to simply be going through the motions, a.k.a. sleepwalking. My team's support, the quality of their work, and overall account management couldn't be compromised in any capacity when my head (and heart) were drifting elsewhere. To that end, I ultimately gravitated toward the world of healthcare.

Fast forward a handful of years later, as a VP of Design at a Fortune 5 healthcare corporation. Within an acquired company, I had some specific goals in this role:

- Building a human-centered design organization from the ground-up: *diverse and inclusive hiring to best represent the world around us, process definition/organizational dependencies*
- Removing outsourced research, growing the practice internally instead: *more nimble, more cost-effective*
- Articulating/implementing the value of design with the organization: *educating the C-suite, collaborating with other leaders to ensure design representation in early/ongoing decision making*
- Impacting our consumer-facing products to ease healthcare burdens across open enrollment, benefits administration, and

life events: *including those we're creating for in the design process, further bringing accessibility to the forefront of our processes*

After around five years, I felt I'd accomplished those goals. And at this point, coasting in the role could've been an option. The design organization was in fantastic shape and well-regarded. We'd made deep inroads with teams and processes to streamline intake and output. My position was secure, the compensation was healthy, and the business was doing well.

All that said, coasting is **not** an option for us. Not as a team member, not as an independent contributor, and beyond a doubt, not in a leadership position. Sleepwalking when you have team members' needs and evolution as your responsibility could be massively detrimental to their support, well-being, and work. A 'from me to we' mindset at the forefront of your self-awareness drives healthy decision-making in this capacity.

In addition, the Director of Research on my team consistently exceeded all of the goals we'd set together and my own expectations. She was beyond ready to take the design organization in new directions and assume more responsibility. Me squatting in the role to collect a paycheck with minimal effort would've stifled her growth and cost the team a brilliant and energized leader. To those ends, I moved on.

an anomali

Lastly and most recently, while working as a Principal Consultant within a consulting firm, I received a call from a former boss, a person I massively respect, trust, and consider a friend. He made me a tantalizing offer: to become the VP of Design within the company he was now a part of, building the design practice and team from the ground up. The associated offer package was impressive, to boot.

Upon reflection and looking at the bigger picture of where I'm at in my career—and in what felt like an affront to the design gods (forgive me, Typographicus)—I turned the offer down. I wasn't fully connected to the prospect of "doing it all over again," so to speak, within a large tech organization and potentially navigating similar political hurdles. I left that world the last time due to my disconnection from the environment—and tech in general.

In fact, the last time I felt fully connected to a company's values and culture was when I was the Design Director at a Swedish design agency. They employed rituals and practices unlike I'd ever seen in the U.S. market. This was my chance to feel that connection once again, and design the environment in which I'd thrive best. To that end—with a mix of fear, exhilaration, and determination—I started my own design consultancy and advisory practice. Across **design leadership**, healthy **culture** advocacy, and working with internal design teams on **craft**, I'd infuse the Swedish cultural sensibilities of egalitarianism, slowing down + pausing with intent, and human connection into the consultancy's DNA.

This stretches my legs across all of my passions and aligns directly with what fulfills me most:

- defining, articulating, and promoting the value of design with organizations, aligning it to their core practices
- coaching and mentoring design leaders to be successful amidst an ever-evolving business landscape
- consulting on healthy culture within business to translate values to actions, defining measurable outcomes, and supporting teams agnostic of the remote or in-person seat. leading / connecting / consulting with internal design teams to create all-living-things-centered project work, agnostic of medium or industry

As I led this book with, I call the business **Anomali** (a word that's Swedish for...well, you can probably guess).

Humble, practical design leadership amongst constant global flux can be challenging to find, often an anomaly. Anomali's mission is to make it plentiful, to bring it to people and organizations who want to embrace real leadership, real design, as part of their mission.

Regarding that job offer from my former boss: at the most fundamental level it distilled down to either doing everything I love on my own terms (with financial risk attached) or doing something very similar to what I'd done previously with an equally nice title and paycheck (minimal financial risk). I put my money where my fulfillment-mouth is.

There's no doubt there's privilege behind being able to make that decision; even at this stage in my career, it's one I'm fortunate to make. What I've described are factors and choices that were bespoke to my specific journey, as all of our journeys are unique. The core drivers behind my clarity, however, are universal:

- An awareness of where I'm most fulfilled, and how I'm best connected to my work
- An understanding of what my values are, and aligning them to my actions
- A recognition of what environment would best support my evolution, and doing my most meaningful work

Over the course of our career's journey as designers, it's a blueprint that serves both us and those we have the privilege to create for. Can we do any less when connection is on the line?

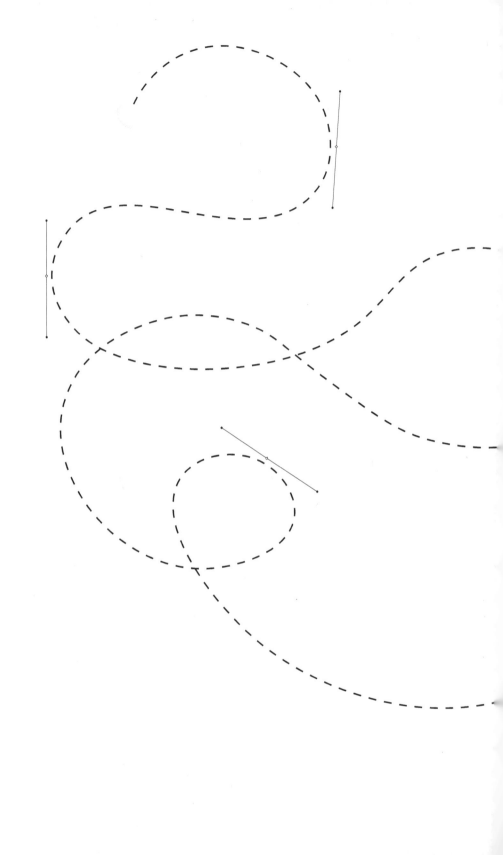

conclusion

Amongst all its associations
and permutations, design is
where we can continue to be
challenged, evolve, thrive, and
make meaningful work.

Why are you a designer?

Did you hesitate in your response? Sometimes the most fundamental question can give us the most unexpected pause. But why?

Our respective design journeys shape our authentic personal narrative along the way. The practices where we thrive provide a spotlight upon what drives us to do what we do. When we leverage humility we're able to not only identify those points of evolution, but seize upon them to our—and our work's—benefit. When your awareness is dialed into those points of connection, *"why are you a designer?"* is a question you'll never hesitate upon again.

Everyone can have their 'meeting introduction' -caliber moment of clarity, as I did way back in this book's opening: when values, actions, work, and environment align. And the best part is, it doesn't have to take you a quarter of a century to obtain.

Design is 'connection.' Design is a profession. It's an interaction, a chair, a community center, and a strategic means of building a team. Amongst all its associations and permutations, design is where we can continue to be challenged, evolve, thrive, and make meaningful work.

So, secure yourself a lovely cup of coffee, close your laptop, and consider: *"am I fulfilled?"* If not, what would it take to get there? We've given you the tools—there's no time like the present to put forth the work to chart that path.

Justin is an internationally reknown design leader, author, and speaker from Chicago.

You'll find him often engaging with the AIGA's speaking events, interviewed in Forbes magazine and Medium's "Forge" publication, and penning articles for Aquent, CEO World Magazine, and A List Apart. He speaks internationally on culture and design, including keynotes at the UXPA International conference, Midwest UX, and St. Louis Design Week. Justin is also the writer of the celebrated book "Creative Culture," a former VP of Design at bswift (a CVS Health company), and the founder of design leadership consultancy Anomali.

anomalibydesign.com

Photo by John Morrison

acknowl-edge-ments

As it turns out, writing a book in the midst of a global pandemic is not a streamlined activity. With two kids (remote learning, then not remote learning, then remote learning again...then not) and two adults working from home concurrently, the focus moments were few and far between. Sometimes, *months*-far in between. This material took far longer than I'd have ever guessed to put to paper and ultimately in your hands, but the stalwart throughout was my incredible partner, best friend, and wife: Kaity. This book would simply not exist without her.

I'm beyond fortunate to have Erika Abrams pen the foreword for this book. She selflessly lent her experience, perspective, and brilliance to introduce this material amidst a busy schedule and a short timeframe.

Jeffrey Zeldman once told me that writing is an incredibly solitary activity—leveraging a strong amount of personal narrative-driven material, I felt that notion in this project far more than the first go around. That said, his kind words, concept and design feedback, and above all else—friendship—once again were priceless. For this second book I again had the incredible fortune to collaborate with editor Ann Maynard, who helped turn my themes from prepackaged cold cuts into filet.

Much of this material was conceived, vetted, and tested via conferece speaking engagements. Great appreciation to the UXPA, AIGA, Big Design, and Leading Design events and attendees for giving me the opportunity to refine these concepts and my messaging. Your candor and feedback was invaluable.

Dan Szuc and Jo Wong have afforded me a consistent creative space (a Sparkle Studio, in fact) since 2018 to go infinitely deeper into my concepts, themes, and personal narrative. These collaborative sessions—often with colleagues from around the world (Kimberly Edgell, Susan J. Wolfe, Greg Evans, Aaron Ginzburg, among them)—have been absolutely paramount toward the nuance and complexity contained within.

My tools: I upgraded across both an iPad Pro and MacBook Pro, respectfully, over the lifespan of this project, making it 4 different devices that helped me wrangle words and set type both in my home office as well as coffee shops. Funnily enough, though, a single sketchbook (and copious pencils) handled the "ugly" stages of ideation and iteration from concept through completion. And what began in a café ultimately concluded in the same one: major thanks to Michelle Martinez and Hero Coffee for hosting my photoshoot, with John Morrison deftly behind the lens.

Lastly—and this is verbatim from *Creative Culture*, but evergreen—thank you to the city of Chicago, my birthplace and home, for serving up unending inspiration through art, music, and culture. Functioning as the backdrop for much of this book's content and interactions, I can't imagine having written it in any other place.

references

chapter 1

"Bring Your Whole Self to Work" by Henna Inam in *Forbes*
https://www.forbes.com/sites/hennainam/2018/05/10/bring-your-whole-self-to-work/?sh=6f28ea6b6291

"Accessibility" by Interaction Design Foundation
https://www.interaction-design.org/literature/topics/accessibility

chapter 2

"Design POV: An In-Depth Look at the Design Industry Now" by AIGA
https://www.aiga.org/aiga-design-pov-reports

Principles of Management
https://open.lib.umn.edu/principlesmanagement/

Creative Culture: Human-Centered Interaction, Design, & Inspiration by Justin Dauer
http://www.the-culturebook.com

Make Meaningful Work: From Sleepwalking to Sparkle by Dan Szuc and Jo Wong
https://www.amazon.com/dp/1737928205

chapter 4

"Episode 9: Designing Health Care Benefits Administration and Corporate Culture with Justin Dauer, VP of Design at bswift" by Pek Pongpaet on *What is UX*

https://whatisux.co/podcast/e9-designing-health-care-benefits-administration-and-corporate-culture-with-justin-dauer-vp-of-design-at-bswift/

"Designing Work That People Love" by Marcus Buckingham in *Harvard Business Review*

https://hbr.org/2022/05/designing-work-that-people-love

chapter 5

"How the Coronavirus Outbreak Has – and Hasn't – Changed the Way Americans Work" by Kim Parker, Juliana Menasce Horowitz, and Rachel Minkin in *Pew Research Center*

https://www.pewresearch.org/social-trends/2020/12/09/how-the-coronavirus-outbreak-has-and-hasnt-changed-the-way-americans-work/

in-fulfillment.com
@in_fulfillment

colophon

Typeset in FF Mark Book, Italic, and Bold, designed by Hannes von Döhren, Christoph Koeberlin, and the FontFont Type Department.

in fulfillment:
the designer's journey

justin dauer

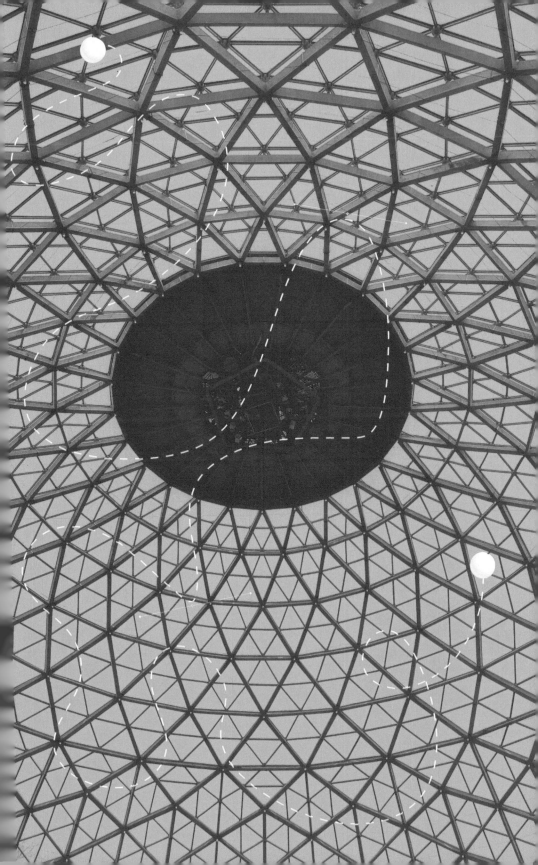

ANDRES
OLIVIA
THE GIRLFRIENDS
THE SPICERS
KATE + BOB
ROY-BROOKS HEINECK 10-11-13
SEP 1990
Carol + Chris 8-17-2012
VICKI
R♥R
FH-AH
John &
E PLOT THICKE
MILLERS 2007
Rachel

Ingram Content Group UK Ltd.
Milton Keynes UK
UKHW052217280623
424229UK00004B/37